ANGELA THOMAS-PHARR

brave

honest questions
women ask

LifeWay Press®
Nashville, Tennessee

Published by LifeWay Press®
© 2011 Angela Thomas
Reprinted September 2018

ISBN 978-1-4158-6956-7
Item 005342722

Dewey decimal classification: 248.843
Subject headings: WOMEN \ FEAR \ CHRISTIAN LIFE

Unless otherwise noted, all Scripture quotations are taken from the Holy Bible, New International Version, copyright © 1973, 1978, 1984 by International Bible Society. Scripture quotations marked AMP are taken from The Amplified® Bible, copyright © 1954, 1958, 1962, 1964, 1965, 1987 by The Lockman Foundation. Used by permission. *www.lockman.org*. Scripture quotations marked HCSB® are taken from the Holman Christian Standard Bible®, copyright © 1999, 2000, 2002, 2003 by Holman Bible Publishers. Used by permission. Scripture quotations marked NASB are taken from the New American Standard Bible®, Copyright © 1960, 1962, 1963, 1968, 1971, 1972, 1973, 1975, 1977, 1995 by the Lockman Foundation. Used by permission. *www.lockman.org*. Scripture quotations marked NCV are taken from the New Century Version®. Copyright © 1987, 1988, 1991 by Thomas Nelson, Inc. Used by permission. All rights reserved. Scripture quotations marked The Message are taken from The Message. Copyright © 1993, 1994, 1995, 1996, 2000, 2001, 2002. Used by permission of NavPress Publishing Group. Scripture quotations marked ESV are taken from The Holy Bible, English Standard Version® (ESV®) Copyright © 2001 by Crossway, a publishing ministry of Good News Publishers. All rights reserved. 2007. Scripture quotations marked NLT are taken from the Holy Bible, New Living Translation, copyright © 1996. Used by permission of Tyndale House Publishers, Inc., Wheaton, IL 60189 USA. All rights reserved.

To order additional copies of this resource, write to LifeWay Church Resources Customer Service; One LifeWay Plaza; Nashville, TN 37234-0113; fax (615) 251-5933; phone toll free (800) 458-2772; order online at *www.lifeway.com*; e-mail *orderentry@lifeway.com*; or visit the LifeWay Christian Store serving you.

Printed in the United States of America

Adult Ministry Publishing
LifeWay Christian Resources
One LifeWay Plaza
Nashville, TN 37234-0152

Contents

About the Author

Angela Thomas -Pharr is a popular national speaker and the best-selling author of 10 books and Bible studies. She is a graduate of the University of North Carolina and Dallas Theological Seminary. Angela has been teaching the Bible for over 25 years using her unique gifts of entertaining storytelling and faithful biblical instruction. Every year she speaks to thousands of women across the United States and around the world. Angela, her husband, four children, and two crazy dogs live in North Carolina.

My sweet friends, welcome to **Brave.**

This study means so much to me personally. Most of my life I have not lived brave, but I have wanted to. Many years I allowed myself to be guided by my insecurities, fears, and what everyone else thought I should do. I have let common distractions deflect me from my goals. I have let others' excuses become mine. I guess I just fell in line and most of the time did what the good, nice people around me were doing and saying.

I am certain God has more. With all my heart, I believe a woman who follows passionately after God can become a brave woman who lives according to His powerful Spirit.

I am even more certain that living brave begins with truth. In the weeks ahead, I hope you'll turn every one of these pages with a longing for truth. I pray the Scriptures become your refuge and strength. I hope you'll be able to say and write the truth of your own needs. Maybe you'll even uncover deeper truths about who you are and how your personal struggles have shaped you.

More than anything, I'm praying you encounter the truths of our God. I long for His character to become glorious to you and a comfort in all that concerns you. In these weeks I pray God will overwhelm you with His goodness, His faithfulness, His enduring love, and His constant affection. Oh my friend, how He loves us. I am convinced He loves you and me. He desires that in His power we will live brave.

By His grace and mercy,
According to the work of the Holy Spirit,
Because of the life of Jesus Christ,
May we become the brave women of God.
With great love and tenderness for you,

Angela

I AM WORN OUT

I had breakfast with my girlfriend yesterday, and she's just worn out.

Her kids aren't babies anymore, but her exhaustion is completely understandable. Her family has been caught in the recession, like most of us, and they have found themselves with three houses, two of them for sale in a poor seller's market. The renter of one just decided to walk away from her lease yesterday. We sat together over pancakes, and I told her I would pray for a miracle. An hour ago she texted, "When it rains, it pours. My college sophomore just lost half his financial aid for next semester. More prayers needed."

Maybe you feel about the same. More prayers needed. Your mind is weary, and the answers are slow. Life just keeps coming.

Maybe you are exhausted, and some of your worn out is physical exhaustion. But for many of us, the heart is numb and the spirit is tired.

It's interesting, when we're just plain tired, like how you feel after a full day of yard work, most of us know what to do with that. Take a good, hot bath. Have a yummy snack. Whisper a tired *amen;* then go to bed early. But when the spirit and mind are worn out, it's so much more difficult to know what to do.

Welcome to our first week of brave questions: God, do You know that I'm worn out? I'm praying that as we seek God together with the truth of our weariness, His character and His answers will become your guide.

As you begin this first day in the first week of our study together, please know that I have prayed for you. I will keep praying for you. God loves the worn-out women. I believe He wants to refresh your soul this week.

Blessings, dear friend.

It is very brave to finally say, "I am not superwoman."

Today is Monday for me. Since it's the first day of this study, maybe it's Monday for you too. I have all the post-weekend symptoms. A full heart from traveling and speaking at a conference and then coming home to scurry around, putting together a combination birthday and Super Bowl party. We had 20 people for dinner and the celebration last night. I loved it all. All the people and the travel and cooking and cleanup. But today is Monday, and once again, doing all the things I love has left me worn out. My head was a little foggy and slow this morning. My jump-to-it attitude took half the day to engage.

Honestly, this is kind of a regular start to a new week. I can only imagine that you begin your Mondays in a similar way. Early this morning, snuggled in my robe and holding my third cup of coffee, I prayed to the Lord, "Oh God, do You know that I am worn out ... again?"

As I have been preparing for our time together this week, I've decided we can experience *worn out* several ways, and I want us to address all of these in the next few days. Obviously physical weariness comes to us, but we can also become weary of our circumstances, emotionally worn out, and especially drained of spiritual strength.

IN WHAT WAYS DO YOU STRUGGLE WITH FEELING WORN OUT?

To me worn out feels like:

Sometimes it literally feels like I have a huge weight pushing down on top of me. A heaviness follows me from room to room. Sometimes it's physical. Sometimes emotional. Sometimes I am too numb to tell the difference.

I am quieter when I'm worn out. My family asks, "Are you OK, Mom?"

In the video this week I'll tell about a question I posted to my Facebook friends. I asked how they'd complete the sentence, "I am worn out because. ..." But let me ask you:

How would you honestly complete these sentences?

I am worn out because:

Here's what worn out makes me feel like:

This is how I usually act and react when I'm worn out:

Maybe after just writing these few responses, you are thinking to yourself, *I don't have time for this Bible study. I'm pooped!* But I believe that this study has divinely found you at the right time, especially this week about worn out. Just so you won't feel alone in your weariness, read with me Proverbs 30:1 in the margin.

The wisdom literature of the Bible declares we will all grow weary. Tired. Worn out. My uncle Donald used to say, "I'm too pooped to pop, just laying here a frying." Maybe a season of "too pooped to pop" has come to you. Honestly, I don't know anyone on this earth who can avoid the inevitable. In these bodies, on this earth, we will know exhaustion in all its varieties. We are the worn-out women.

NO SUPERWOMEN

Maybe some women are more organized. Maybe some live inside stronger bodies. But the truth of our humanity is that no superwomen exist on this earth. We each have been created by God, fully human and walking around with human needs and human frailties. Today my humanity reminds me of several things:

I can't eat the way I used to—four pieces of white bread for an afternoon snack. Careless eating makes me feel bad. When I feel bad, worn out isn't far behind. If I ate all that yummy bread today, I'd be doubled over with a stomachache the rest of the night. My humanity can be a drag.

I need about seven hours of sleep every night. Eight is even better. When I get to the lobby at 4 a.m. to make the first flight out of town, my body will require payback, somehow, some way. I call it "crazy tax." I can make crazy choices and push myself to get more crammed into a few days. But crazy tax is always coming. I am human.

My brain turns off right about 8:00 in the evening. I tell you, it goes to mush.

I take all kinds of vitamins trying to extend its daily reach, but nope, I can't seem to force many brainwaves after 8:00 p.m.

How about you? How does your humanity remind you that you can't be superwoman?

Facing my limitations and weakness forces me to do a few things. First, I have to put my faith in God. Again and again and again. He can take care of all that I cannot stay awake to worry about.

He is the One who meets every need. He is Lord and Sovereign in this universe. Oh, can I tell you how very thankful I am that He is God of all and I am not? I have squarely and firmly put my faith in His ability to run the planet. He is able.

Does finding yourself worn out tend to cause you to trust God more or to lose hope when your strength runs out?

"My God will supply all your needs according to His riches in glory in Christ Jesus."

—

Philippians 4:19, HCSB

Second, my limitations force me to prioritize. After my relationship with God, my order goes: Marriage, children, and ministry. That's it. I truly have no room for anything else. I'd like to add lots of fun things such as cooking classes, gardening, and home design. But my humanity has forced me to choose what matters most. For now, in this season of life, I can give priority to my big three. Most everything else is pushed to a very distant fourth.

What would you list as your Big Three?

1.
2.
3.

Just for fun, what would you love to add to your life one day, when it's time for your priorities to change?

How do you feel about having to sacrifice fun things because of responsibilities?

So, here we have it, our first day of being worn out together. Welcome to the club. Not a superwoman in the room. Just us, human, so very aware we are in over our heads. Asking God if He sees. I can tell you this at the very beginning: God is not mad. The Creator is very well acquainted with our design.

> ## "For he knows how we are formed, he remembers that we are dust."
>
> — Psalm 103:14

We are just beginning to consider the truth of our condition before God. I pray that today you know that you are not alone. My worn-out heart sighs from my truth, "Oh, how very much I need a Savior."

Oh, Jesus, come be our Savior. Our Rescuer. Our Provider. Our Friend. I know You see that I am worn and weary. So I am bringing my truth to You today. My weariness is laid on Your altar. I have nowhere else to go. No one else can save me. I've come to You with my great need. Teach me. Show me. Hold me. Keep saving me. I love You. Very amen and amen.

DAY 2

This morning I'm flying from Cape Town to Johannesburg, South Africa. The Middle Eastern man sitting beside me was asleep before they even closed the door. I am smiling as I type because he had propped his sleepy head up with his hand, but his arm just fell down and his whole body jerked him back upright. Still dead asleep. I've done that.

What is interesting is that I'm on a plane with people from many nations. Most of us don't speak the same language. I hear conversations all around me, and I can only understand a few words here and there. But as I look into the eyes of my fellow passengers, I see a universal language of the soul. You don't need a translator to know the person in front of you is worn out, weary, and even discouraged. I don't know their stories or how they came to such weariness, but their eyes and countenance say it all. People are weary and worn out the world over.

The Bible is very clear about these thoughts. We all will become tired in some way, in some season. No one is exempt. The Scripture gives several observations about our weariness. Let's examine what God says about how we become so tired.

work makes you tired

No big shock here. Whew, I'm so glad to know that the Bible says that work makes you tired.

> ## "She has wearied herself with toil."
>
> Ezekiel 24:12, esv

This may sound a little crazy to you, but that actually gives me comfort. God knows that good work makes a good woman good and tired. Wiped out. Flat as a pancake. Work is supposed to make you tired. It's how we're supposed to feel when we've given all we have to take care of our families or to finish a big assignment or to get to the other side of final exams. We're supposed to be tired.

Sometimes, just before I fall asleep, I will whisper to God: "This is how I'm supposed to feel when I've done good, hard work. Thank You for this good tired. Amen ... zzz."

You see, we won't ever get to some spiritual place where we balance just right and delegate just right and never experience weary or worn out again. Honestly, I think if you get there, you may be forsaking some really great work God is calling you to do.

So, where does your good tired come from these days?

For you, what distinguishes good-work tired from all the other ways we feel worn out?

ANXIOUS TOIL MAKES YOU EVEN MORE TIRED.

Good work differs from the kind of unscriptural exhaustion that comes from "anxious toil." I bet you already know the difference in your heart.

What makes for "anxious toil" in your life, and how does it feel to you?

Do any of these words apply to some part of your life?

Circle your choice(s).

fretful   jumpy   worried   striving

tense   fearful   on edge   in a tizzy

overloaded   faithless   nervous

manipulating

Want to go a little deeper today?

Have a little extra time? Read the whole Book of Ecclesiastes, and pay special attention to Solomon's description of life "under the sun." What if we learned to live above the sun, seeing as God sees, thinking more like He thinks? Where are you living?

Solomon, the writer of Ecclesiastes, used the phrase "under the sun" to consider a life lived apart from God or apart from His leading. Maybe we could think of a life centered on God as a life that is looking above the sun. It's a beautiful picture, don't you think? The life underneath the sun can't see like God sees. Doesn't have the big picture. Only sees what's underneath the clouds. Doesn't ever factor in the sovereignty of God. I can picture that hunched over, fretful, "under the sun" woman right now. I've been that woman, so I actually know her intimately.

What if we learned to live "above the sun," seeing as God sees, thinking more like He thinks?

Solomon said that when we live "under the sun," everything is meaningless, toil is exhausting, and the striving is endless. His exact words actually go like this, "All is vanity." (See Eccl. 1:2, NASB.) Ecclesiastes is 12 chapters woven with this same thread. Solomon wanted us to get it. If you are living "under the sun," without a God-perspective and a God-focus, then really, life is just meaningless. Psalm 127 calls the kind of work that we do apart from God's leading "anxious toil."

"It is in vain that you rise up early and go late to rest, eating the bread of anxious toil; for he gives to his beloved sleep" (Ps. 127:2, ESV).

As God followers, we are to live above the sun. Where God is. Thinking like God thinks. Doing what God has called us to do. Viewing this life in the light of eternity.

Look at this scale and put an x where it feels like you are living today.

I realize that it's so easy to let our perspective slide. Lord knows, we just flat-out forget. Before we realize it, our heart has fallen into anxiousness, our work has become anxious, and our focus has turned from God. We are just exhausted.

How would you advise a younger believer to turn her heart back toward God and begin to live above the sun again?

"Of making many books there is no end, and much study wearies the body."

—
Ecclesiastes
12:12

Smile.
This one I'm taking
as a personal
reminder to keep my
work above the sun.

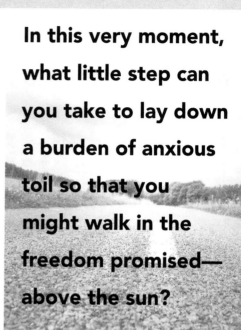

In this very moment, what little step can you take to lay down a burden of anxious toil so that you might walk in the freedom promised— above the sun?

GRIEF EXHAUSTS THE BODY AND SOUL.

Almost everyone I know has experienced the pure exhaustion that comes to us from grief. The psalmist said: "I am worn out from sobbing. All night I flood my bed with weeping, drenching it with my tears. My vision is blurred by grief; my eyes are worn out" (Ps. 6:6-7, NLT).

We can know great sorrow over our losses, our circumstances, and even our own choices. The soul grieves for many reasons, but the Bible is so clear: Grief empties us of strength. It will completely wear us out.

A woman at my Bible study said to me last week, "Thanks for saying that. I lost my husband three months ago, and I have never been more exhausted in my life. I finally have the words to say what it is: 'I am exhausted from my grief,' and God knows that this awful grief has worn me out."

Tell me about the last time you felt E X H A U S T E D because of grief.

Grief makes you tired.
Robs you of strength. Wearies your heart, soul, and mind.

SIN MAKES YOU TIRED.

The prophet Jeremiah said, "They weary themselves with sinning" (9:5). If you've ever watched people choosing blatant sin, you know it's true—they wear themselves out. Maybe you keep living around your sin and trying to hide it. Maybe the prophet's words ring loud in your soul and your head shouts a silent "Amen" because you know

firsthand that sin does make you tired. Oh so very tired.

Honestly, if you are weary and worn out and you can't exactly figure out why, here is the first place I would look. Is there sin in your life you've been trying to live with? Are there sin patterns you've been meaning to deal with?

A few years ago I encountered a woman who was caught in a web of lies. Almost every interaction with her involved yet another silly lie and stories she had to keep straight. Just 10 minutes with her wore me out. I believe that poor woman must surely be exhausted from her own sin patterns.

Here's a little space for you to stop and consider. I don't want you to keep reading or zoom past this small part of today's study. But just for a moment ask God, "Am I clean?"

Close your eyes for a few minutes and sit with the question in front of God. "Am I clean?"

Brave women turn to God when they are weary.

I have never known God to speak to me from His wrath. He always prompts me toward purity with gentleness and love. Sit and listen to the gentle voice of God. He can tell you if there is sin that makes you tired.

I think we're becoming friends by now. I am propped up on my hotel bed in Johannesburg praying for you right this minute.

Father, come with Your gentle presence to each one of my friends. Minister to the worn-out women who have just begun to seek You for their weariness. Teach each one of us where to turn and what to do with our weary. We love You so much. We need You so much.

So very amen and amen.

DAY 3

This world, oh my goodness, this world will tell you lies. Come here when you're tired, and we'll refresh your body. Do that when you are weary, and your heart will jump for joy. Buy that cream. Send away for those vitamins. Run to a bottle. Hide in the dark. Jump through the next hoop. Google™ for another answer. On and on it goes. The world shouts to each one of us its prescription for weariness. I have listened too many times to this lying world and counted on its answers. I bet you have too.

I believe the big question for us this week is this: "Where do you go with your weary?" Truly, where do you turn when you're tired? your bed? a carton of ice cream? the gym? a bottle of wine? I am a girl who wears out in the normal, human being kinds of ways. I assume that you are too. I could run a million places or do a million things, but I'm certain no one and no thing can give what the heart truly craves. We need a rest that only God can give.

What would you say are

three places women most often turn with their weariness?

1.
2.
3.

Hear me say something clearly: We can do great things in this world to live in strength, wisdom, and courage. Lord knows most of us are trying everything. But here is the big, hairy truth: Many of us are doing great worldly things to care for ourselves and yet not living with an inside strength to counter our soul weariness.

It is so very brave to turn with your weariness and to ask of God, "Do You know that I'm worn out?" My prayer is that you will begin to hear the Lord respond to your heart, "Do you know I am your God who does not grow weary?" Our God is not like us. Hal-le-lu-jah!

What's a woman who loves God supposed to do? How about this?

Turn to God first.

Then do everything in wisdom to care for your body, soul, and mind.

He does not become weary or wear out or fall flat or even need a nap.
He is not a big grandpa in the sky nodding off in His easy chair.
HE IS GOD!
And God, in His very nature, is different from you and me.
He does not need to be physically replenished.
He does not need anything from outside Himself to be a better, stronger God.
His character is self-sustaining.

I only say this because too many times I've reversed the order. I have tried to find the wisdom apart from God. I write about it today because I guess you've done the same thing too.

Let's stop for a minute and observe Isaiah 40:28-31.

Take out your pen or highlighter, and for some of you colored-pen girls, here's your place to really mark it up.

1. First, underline or highlight every character trait of God that you read in this passage.

2. Second, circle the gifts of God to the weary, His promises to us.

3. Third, draw a big star or highlight with all your colors or do whatever your creative heart can do to make this next truth stand out. Look at the passage and tell me how God transfers His very character to the weary and the weak.

"Do you not know? Have you not heard? The LORD is the everlasting God, the Creator of the ends of the earth. He will not grow tired or weary, and his understanding no one can fathom. He gives strength to the weary and increases the power of the weak. Even youths grow tired and weary, and young men stumble and fall; but those who hope in the LORD will renew their strength. They will soar on wings like eagles; they will run and not grow weary, they will walk and not be faint" (Isa. 40:28-31).

Did you find the transfer of God's strength? Still not quite sure? OK, here's your hint: The transfer happens right after the word "but." Do you see it now? The holy transfer of God's character happens when we come into His presence and put our "hope in the LORD." Right there. Boom. That's it. There's your answer. Where do we run with our weary? The Scriptures tell us to run to God and put our hope in His promises.

Now list with me the benefits of placing your hope in God.

I'll get you started.

I will *renew my strength.*

I will *soar on wings like eagles.*

I will *run.*

I will _____.

I will _____.

I will _____.

My friend, here is where we go with our weary: to the only One who can transfer the strength of His character into our bodies and souls. Here is the truth you cannot miss: A hope firmly centered on the Lord renews our strength.

In this passage, the word "renew" means "to exchange," like taking off old clothes and putting on new ones. When we put our hope in God, He is able to exchange our weakness for His power. Where is your hope today? Most of us know the right answer, but still, it's easy to misplace our hope in the blur of living on this earth. I have mistakenly placed my hope in some of the following things:

As you read my list, note any way you have duplicated my "misplaces." I've trusted ...

> myself or my skill set
> my determination or
>   willpower
> my parents
> my children
> my husband
> my health
> calm circumstances
> financial contracts
> the real estate market
> the promises of the
>   well-meaning
> my leaders
> my government

Do you have any more ideas that you could add to my false hope list?

Isaiah said that those who hope in the Lord will renew their strength. Other translations say "they who wait for the LORD" (ESV), which is an idea we see woven throughout Scripture. *The Message* paraphrases this another way:

"But those who wait upon GOD get fresh strength."
ISAIAH 40:31

Today I want you to remember that God knows our propensity to become weary. It's built into the very fabric of our humanity. But God has made a way for us to know fresh strength. He has provided a means to make a holy and mysterious transfer of His character to our souls when we come into His presence and place our hope in the truth of who He is.

DAY 4

A brave woman receives God's gifts for her weariness.

Hey all you worn-out women, today I want to remind you of some really great news. You can trade your worn-out spirit for fresh, new strength. Your weary heart can be restored. Our God, who does not grow weary, has made a way for you and for me.

Your Creator gets you. He understands your crazy life. He knows that you work until exhaustion. He sees how many people need your time, your input, and your energy. He is completely aware of your design. God cares for His worn-out girls. Really and truly He does.

God's compassion toward us is not only consistent and faithful but it is unfailing. Without interruption. Steady. Reliable. Promised and sure.

According to the Scriptures, God has made beautiful provisions for the worn out.

He has always known our great need, and in His Word we learn how He makes a way for our help and restoration. I'm praying that today you will make some everyday life decisions based on the provisions of God for your body, soul, and mind.

I want us to walk through eight lessons concerning God's provisions for the worn out. He is not mad about your weakness. He doesn't keep His distance because you've grown tired. He's not wringing His hands about your failings.

Our God has made a way to renew our strength. For the rest of today's study, we'll walk through several lessons of Scripture that have ministered to me. My list is not exhaustive (pun intended), but hopefully these thoughts will suggest a beginning toward understanding the heart of God toward the weary.

1.

THE PRESENCE OF GOD RESTORES.

How do you do with the mysterious? When I was younger, I didn't handle mystery so well. I wanted answers, logic, and a formula. The older I get, the more excited I am about trusting the things I can't control or understand about the nature of God. The Bible says we see through a mirror dimly. We only know in part. God is divine, and I am not. So this issue falls into that category. No formula captures God. I only know that what the Bible says is true. God says that when we come to Him, He restores the soul and provides rest for the weary.

Which particular aspect of Matthew 11:28 gives you hope or encouragement?

What does this verse tell us to do?

What does the verse promise?

God obviously promises a physical rest for your weariness and a soul rest from your heavy burdens. But Jesus required an action on our part.

What do you sense God is saying to you from the verse?

Are you weary? In what everyday kind of way can you get to God today? Maybe you could choose one of these suggestions:

- ❀ Bow your head where you are.
- ❀ Push all your books aside, and physically just lie in the presence of God.
- ❀ Turn off every distraction until stillness surrounds you.

What one specific action could you choose to take to "come to" Him?

> *"Come to me, all of you who are weary and burdened, and I will give you rest."*
>
> —
>
> MATTHEW 11:28

2.

MANY TIMES WE EXPERIENCE A DIVINE WAIT BEFORE REFRESHMENT.

Many times in Scripture we read about the one who drags himself into the presence of God and then waits. The psalmist said:

> "We wait in hope for the LORD."
>
> PSALM 33:20

I don't pretend to understand the details of God's heart, but I do know that sometimes He desires that we wait in His presence until we receive His refreshment. We wait for strength. We wait for guidance. We wait for healing. Something powerful and life-giving comes through the waiting. This falls into the category of learning to trust our God of wonder and mystery.

Do you remember a time of waiting for God to renew your soul? Tell me about the circumstances.

Have you seen God's goodness through your own situation?
○ yes ○ no ○ I'm not sure

If so, how long did you have to wait to see God's goodness shine through, and how did you eventually see it?

During my separation and divorce I vividly remember long, long months filled with the blackest nights of waiting on God. No answers. No direction. All I knew was He was my only hope. People would say to me, "God is coming." And I believed them, but in my spirit I could not sense any answers. The waiting seemed to last much longer than I felt I could endure and was darker than I ever imagined darkness could be.

Now I can testify to an amazing truth. God came. He came to rescue my soul from its darkest night. He came to carry my worn-out body and my worn-out kids. As a bonus, God continues to bring light from that time to give refreshment and strength I would not have known without the waiting.

3.

THE SABBATH REST IS GOD'S GIFT TO US.

Hebrews 4 elevates the idea of Sabbath to proclaim our rest from dead works. Our entire walk with Christ is a Sabbath rest because He is our righteousness.

> "There remains, then, a Sabbath-rest for the people of God; for anyone who enters God's rest also rests from his own work, just as God did from his."
>
> HEBREWS 4:9-10

To observe the Sabbath we should worship the Lord and rest from our work. I also believe the Sabbath should be kept every week, not just when we get around to it every few months.

My job is to study and read and to move words around, trying to communicate an ancient truth in a brand-new way. On the Sabbath I rest from my work and all the words and studying. To make dinner for my family is a joy for me. It restores me. I believe I have permission from God to enjoy what feels like rest for me.

From what do you sense God would have you rest so you can receive the gift of His Sabbath for your soul?

I AM
El Elyon,
the God
most high.

I AM
*Jehovah
Shammah,*
the Lord is
now here.

I AM
*the Lord
of the Sabbath,*
the God of all,
even the gift
of the Sabbath.

I AM
refuge.
God is our haven.

the **I AM'**s of God

When Moses asked for God's name, God replied, I AM THAT I AM or I AM WHAT I AM—a title expressing God's self-existence and His unchangeable character.

He always was what He is, He is what He was, He will ever be what He was and is. With Him there is no changing.

In this study, I pray you hear God asking the question back to you, "Do you know who I AM?" Do you know His unchanging character toward you? I pray you learn a little more every day about the great character of our God who is I AM.

4.

JESUS DID NOT HEAL EVERYONE OR GO TO EVERY TOWN.

What can you cut out of your life that's making you tired? Even good things need to go if they are standing in the way of what God has called you to.

In our video session this week we'll talk about Dr. Martin, who challenged me that Jesus did not heal every person who was sick or minister to everyone He saw. Dr. Martin said, "Jesus only did what His Father instructed Him to do, and so should you."

Thank you, Dr. Martin, for a Scripture truth that gives boundaries to my purpose and a perspective to my abilities. Jesus didn't do everything, and I can't do everything, even if I give it my best shot. God is calling me to go only as He guides. Sweet words of restraint. Words of rest for your soul and mine. End your day with a moment of introspection. Without beating yourself up, how do you need to apply Dr. Martin's words to your life?

L et's begin today in prayer. I'll start. You close.

God, thank You for permission to consider my weakest places and truthfully bring them to You. I've told myself not to think about my weakness. Just cover it up and move on. But God, I truly need answers. I need to know what a worn-out woman is supposed to do. I want to know You. Hear from You. Follow You. I want to be brave. Lord, please show me Your promises for worn-out women like me.

Yesterday we looked at four of the provisions God has made in Scripture for the worn out. Let's pick back up there today. God has made a way for us and here's more.

5.
JESUS REQUIRED PHYSICAL, MENTAL, AND EMOTIONAL REST.

Keep the context in mind. Jesus, the Son of God, divine in nature, perfect in all His ways, without sin and without flaw. Even our divine Jesus, when He poured Himself into the confines and restrictions of our humanity, needed rest. Human beings require rest. Our Creator wove the need into our DNA. Many times the Scriptures note Jesus' need for rest.

How does Jesus' need for rest help you to recognize your own need for rest?

Sometimes we find ourselves trying to imitate a guest on a talk show or organize our lives around an article in a magazine. The Bible says we are called to be imitators of Christ.

"Follow my example, as I follow the example of Christ."
1 Corinthians 11:1

Today, not tomorrow, how might you incorporate just a taste of this rest into your day?

"Then Jesus said, 'Let's go off by ourselves to a quiet place and rest awhile.' He said this because there were so many people coming and going that Jesus and his apostles didn't even have time to eat."

—

Mark 6:31, NLT

6.

REPENTANCE LEADS TO REFRESHING.

Don't we all know what it feels like to be free of a sin, even just a little one? Remember the last time you asked and received someone's forgiveness? Ahhh, the freedom of having done the right thing, even if it stings in the process. There's a lightness in the forgiven soul. A refreshing and great, great joy that comes to our spirit.

The Lord's refreshing is not just a one-time event at salvation. Being cleansed of our sin gives refreshment to our weary souls over and over all throughout our journey. And so, my sister, is there anything inside you that needs repentance? I know you long for the Lord's refreshment, so take a personal inventory with God. Is there anything that keeps you unclean?

"Repent, then, and turn to God, so that your sins may be wiped out, that times of refreshing may come from the Lord."

—

Acts 3:19

Could you tell me about a time when you repented of something you hardly thought you could live without—or with—and God sent you a season of refreshing?

◯ yes ◯ no

If so, describe how quickly or slowly the time of refreshing came.

I'm just thinking as I'm writing, *Who really wants to write their sin on lines for anyone else to see?* There is no need to do that. There will be no lines here. Just bow your head and receive God's forgiveness and refreshment for every repentance.

7.

IF YOU WALK IN THE GOOD WAY, YOUR SOUL WILL REST.

I know I'm gonna sound so old school here. It's not really cool or hip to say what I'm going to say. But it turns out,

> when you live good
>   and act good
>   and choose good,
>   rest for your soul results.

See, I told you being good is not cool. Cool is edgy, aloof, secretive, mysterious—you know, stuff like that. But the Bible says:

"Stand by the roads, and look, and ask for the ancient paths, where the good way is; and walk in it, and find rest for your souls."

JEREMIAH 6:16, ESV

So what if we take good back? Redeem it. Make good cool again. There is rest in walking the good way. I want all the rest that a good life will bring!

8.

GODLY FRIENDS REFRESH YOUR SOUL.

My soul refresher is Carlye. She has the gift. A few minutes on the phone with her and none of my circumstances have changed, but my soul is always refreshed. **Do you have a soul refresher? Or maybe two? You can write their names here.**

If you don't have a soul-refreshing friend, would you write a prayer asking God to bring you one or to bring you to someone who needs such a friend?

When Paul wrote to the church in Corinth he said that his friends Stephanas, Fortunatus, and Achaicus "have refreshed my spirit and yours. You should recognize the value of people like these" (1 Cor. 16:18, NCV). Maybe in a lifetime we meet two or three people who refresh our souls. Paul said we should recognize the value of people like these. I think recognizing their value means that we do a few things.

- ✿ We carve out time for godly friendship, even when there is distance involved.
- ✿ We let them know in thoughtful ways how much they mean to us.
- ✿ We give to them as they have given to us by listening, remembering, laughing.

While we're at it, as the Holy Spirit is really convicting me in the moment: Am I a soul refresher? for my husband? my children? the neighbor down the street? Oh may it be.

I pray that both of us will know friendships on this earth that restore and refresh the soul. I also pray that we will be able to give even more than we have received.

OUR FINAL REST, HALLELUJAH!

This week we've spent days bringing our weariness to God and learning that His character is so very different from ours. He is our God who does not grow weary. Not only does He never tire but also He makes so many beautiful provisions to us, the worn out, in the truths of Scripture. Maybe God has saved the best for last because the Bible promises that one day every person who follows Jesus Christ will step from this world into our final rest. Can I hear all the worn-out women shout "Hallelujah!"?

One day our setting will match our longing. We will live at peace, inside and out, forever and ever. Every time I teach this truth, my eyes fill with tears. It's the same right now as I'm typing. I really think I'm content and blessed and living in the fullness of God's peace for me on this earth, and yet, when I consider my final rest in heaven, I cry. My soul longs to go home.

Even though I love my life, those tears leak out and tell the truth of my soul. I was made for the presence of God. I was made for the rest He promises this weary soul. And as much as I love my family and this world, this woman will be so happy to get home. To finally be where I belong. I'm going home to heaven one day, and I will enjoy my rest there forever.

Think of an ongoing burden you bear. How does it change your perspective if you reframe that situation with the awareness that this life is short but heaven is forever?

No truth speaks more powerfully to the worn out. We're going home.

Until then, my fellow traveler, I pray we remember how great our God is and that the Bible makes a way for us, gives a grace to the weary. I pray that we take God at His word and begin to live everything we have learned this week.

> If you have bravely asked God,
> "Do You know that I'm worn out?"
> I pray you hear His voice speak to you.

Do you know I AM your God who does not grow weary?

My worn-out daughter, lift up your eyes to the hills and see that your help comes from Me, the One who made you. I AM the Maker of heaven and earth. I AM He, the One who will not let your foot slip. I will watch over you, and I will not slumber while you sleep. No, I will neither slumber nor sleep whether you wake or sleep.

I will refresh your tired body, and I will restore your tired soul. Come and wait for Me so that I can give you fresh strength. I want you to run and not become weary, walk and not be faint.

Follow the model of My Son, Jesus. Learn to take time for your soul. Wear His yoke, not this world's. Keep a Sabbath day to refresh your body, spirit, and soul.

You are my brave beloved, and I AM your God who does not grow weary.

Forever and ever, amen.

My very brave friend, I pray you find new rest in knowing our God who is I AM. And this very night, I hope you sleep sweet, tucked underneath the covering of our God who loves you dearly. This mama finds so much peace in knowing I am held, even in my weakness, by a God whose strength is everlasting.

Let us put our hope in Him.

Zzzzzz.

I am worn out because

_____.

It is a _____ of this life to believe that we will get to a place one day where we will not grow weary and we will not wear out.

Thankfully, God is _____ like us.

"Those _____ _____ in the Lord will renew their strength" (Isa. 40:31).

Eight Provisions for the Worn-Out Woman

1. The _____ of God restores.

2. Sometimes we experience a divine _____ before refreshment.

3. The _____ _____ is God's gift to us.

4. Jesus did not _____ everyone or _____ everywhere.

5. Jesus required physical, _____, and _____ rest.

6. _____ leads to refreshing.

7. If you walk in the _____ way, your soul will rest.

8. Godly _____ restore your soul.

The lines, "I am weary, O God; I am weary, O God, and worn out" appear only in the ESV translation of Proverbs 30:1.
Angela quotes from Gladstone, Jennie M. Bingham, "By Way of Illustration," in *Sunday School Journal*, Vol. 31, (New York: Eaton & Mains Publishers, Methodist Publishing House, 1899), 716.

Video sessions are available for download at *www.lifeway.com/women*

i am suffering a
thorn

Tomorrow I will begin writing this week's Bible study about suffering a thorn, but tonight God has been dealing with me about our next five days. I began by asking the Lord, "How can I introduce this topic in a way that will draw the women's hearts?" Because, really, who wants to spend a week on a topic nobody wants to experience? All night the Lord has reminded me this week is for you.

You may be suffering a thorn this very minute. This week's study is for you.

You may have no idea what a thorn is. This week's study is for you.

You may love someone who bears a thorn. This week's study is for you.

I taught this material in Africa and here in my hometown, and both times this message powerfully impacted the women in the room. So I believe the Holy Spirit is prompting me to lean into God even more fully for this week's writing. I have no idea what God will do in your heart or with the women in your small group, but I believe this week of ministry can be powerful.

I hope this doesn't sound hokey or hyperspiritual to you, but I believe God is asking me to fast for your thorn while I write this week of the study. Fasting always makes me more tenderhearted, and I've already come to this topic a bit frail from my own thorn, so we'll see what God is up to.

And so my friend, would you start with me in prayer?

O Father, for each of us, wherever we are as we study this passage, please come with Your beautiful presence of sufficiency and grace. Please minister renewed strength to my sister by the power of the Holy Spirit. Heal and comfort every woman who needs more of You. And according to Your will, please remove the thorns and end the suffering.

In the sweet name of Jesus, amen.

essentially it was something like *You Can't Kill This Thing Even If You Try.* So I bought it, asked my husband to dig the hole, lamented because we didn't have special dirt to put around the roots, and then worried because we were probably planting my one shot at roses all wrong.

Turns out that the tag was right. Not only is my bush still living but it's thriving. The plant is still small but covered with blooms everywhere!

THE PAIN OF A THORN

I have one little rose bush in my backyard, mostly because everyone said roses are difficult to grow and require a lot of time so I should never attempt them. Daylilies, that's what I'm supposed to plant. No attention required for beautiful summer color. But I still can't resist looking at the roses every time I go to a nursery.

What do you know? One day my local farmer's market had the rose bush for me. I can't remember the name on the tag, but

Just a few minutes ago I walked out to my strong-willed little experiment with some clippers. I thought I'd cut some roses to put on my desk while I write the study about thorns. Now here is the silly part. My rose bush is so young that as I was clipping I decided my super-duper rosebush must not have any thorns because my little buds just seemed to have nubs instead of thorns. *Wonderful*, I thought! I have a thriving thornless little bush of roses. Then I stuck my hand down a little farther. Ouch! You guessed it; there were plenty of thorns, just not on top where I could see.

The thorns were underneath where I hadn't yet looked. Now I'm typing with two thorn pricks in my fingers. I only wanted to look at a few thorns for some kind of literary inspiration, not dab away drops of blood because I felt them, but that is the problem with thorns. They hide unseen, and no one ever wants to feel the jab of their pain.

The apostle Paul wrote this about his thorn:

"To keep me from becoming conceited because of these surpassingly great revelations, there was given me a thorn in my flesh, a messenger of Satan, to torment me. Three times I pleaded with the Lord to take it away from me. But he said to me, 'My grace is sufficient for you, for my power is made perfect in weakness.' "

2 CORINTHIANS 12:7-9

Theologians have long speculated about the nature of Paul's thorn in this passage. Most seem to agree that it was some kind of physical affliction, although no one really knows for sure. Some have speculated Paul's thorn was an incessant temptation or relentless opponent to his ministry.

I began to pray for you last night, and my first prayer was that you might have no idea what I'm talking about. I hope you're scratching your head and saying out loud, "What in the world is a thorn?" But I have met many women, and I've heard too many stories. What I know is that many of us are suffering the pain of a thorn.

No matter where you find yourself, I hope you'll stay with me for this week's study. Whether you are called to bear a thorn, called to love one who does, or both, the power of God's Word can do a transforming work in your soul.

Which box or boxes would you check about thorns?

☐ Angela, I have **no idea** what you're talking about!

☐ **I have known** the pain of a thorn, but thankfully it is now removed.

☐ I am **currently suffering** with a thorn.

☐ **I love someone who is** suffering, and my heart breaks for her pain.

I believe that for a season and perhaps for the rest of my life on this earth, God has called me to suffer with a thorn. With regard to my own thorn, I'll just tell you what I feel is appropriate. My thorn is a relationship that might best be described as an adversary. I shouldn't say anymore, and I hope you understand. I don't mean to be vague, but I have to let that description stand.

What I can tell you is that I do not want this thorn. I wish with everything in me that God would remove this awful, plaguing hurt. I am weary of its place in my life. But that is the thing about a thorn. No one wants it. If I could reach down and remove it myself, I would. I have grown to hate its awful torment. And yet I can do absolutely nothing to make it go away. It is a thorn in my flesh until God decides to remove it or until I stand in glory, finally free.

Do you struggle with a thorn in your life? Or maybe a thorn in your past has been removed. What is or was your thorn?

How long have you suffered with this thorn?

My thorn has made me feel many awful emotions. Anger. Torment. Resentment. Bitterness. Vengefulness. Numbness.

> The brave woman asks God to remove her thorn, even as she learns to accept its presence.

As you think through your thorn-journey,
with what feelings have you dealt? On your list, circle the thorn-related emotions you still feel.

When we talk about the apostle Paul suffering a thorn, it seems "apostle-like" and noble. He was a great Christ follower. His life and teachings have guided all the Christ followers who came after him. But maybe you feel like me. I am just a girl from North Carolina. I'm not an apostle. My thorn is not noble. Even so, it is a thorn I have been called to bear. It's likely you don't feel your thorn is noble either.

Do you ever just feel like shouting, "Whyyyyy? Why this thorn? Why me? What did I do to qualify for the all-time deepest, irremovable, sharpest thorn ever? Lord, do You know that I'm suffering a thorn here?"

Do you remember a time you asked why?

I truthfully haven't ever received an answer for my WHY question. If you have, what was the answer?

Honestly, knowing that Paul suffered a thorn has never really given me any comfort about mine.

I want to follow Christ with every fiber of my being. I will follow Him even with the soul-limp of this thorn, but for me there is no comfort in belonging to The Thorn Club.

The only comfort I have ever received comes from God's response to Paul: "My grace is sufficient for you, for my power is made perfect in weakness" (2 Cor. 12:9).

God said to Paul and He says to us today: I AM sufficient.

That means without my understanding all the whys and even without my coopera-tion, God's grace for my thorn is sufficient. His grace is enough for my circumstances, and He continues to be enough whether or not I choose to believe Him. My comfort has come when I have finally believed and settled it in my soul … God is enough.

El Shaddai: Hebrew scholars teach us that one of the Old Testament names for God, *El Shaddai,* is a composite term of *sha* ("the one who") and *dai* ("is sufficient").[1]

We've got four more days with this topic, and we'll talk more about God's grace on day 5, but I'd love to know now—where are you with believing God's grace is sufficient? Sometimes the thorn is so evil and hurtful that it takes a while for us to get to God's grace. Has it been that way with you? Do you have the peace that comes from believ-ing God's grace is sufficient, or do you still need to get there?

Tell me how you have struggled in believing God's grace is sufficient even in your pain.

I AM

I AM *El Shaddai.*
The almighty, all-sufficient God

I AM Comfort.
God is our Protector and Comforter.

I AM *Jehovah-Elohim.*
The majestic, omnipotent God

I AM a Fortress.
God is our defense.

I AM a Shield.
God is a Preserver and Protector of His children.

I hate to tell you, but this week isn't about five easy steps to thorn removal. I wish it were. Our week together is about the thorns life brings, but more importantly, it is about the character of God. It takes a brave woman to ask the Lord, "Do You know that I'm suffering a thorn?" and an even braver one to receive His truth, "Do you know I am the all-sufficient God?"

As I continue praying for all of us, you can know that at the top of my prayer list I am asking God to remove our thorns. He does that, you know. In His time, according to His will, God does remove thorns. But for those of us who will get to the end of this book still suffering a thorn, I am praying that the covering of God's grace will come to us as the sweetest comfort we have ever known. If I'm going to have to walk around with this thorn for the rest of my days, then I want to live bravely right in the face of the very thing I never wanted to endure.

May God's all-sufficient grace comfort you now. I'm asking the Lord not to wait but to begin pouring out His sufficiency on you even before you ask.

El Shaddai, come and be I AM in the heart of every woman who reads this page. So very amen and amen.

THE BARBS OF A THORN

PART ONE

A few weeks ago I taught this message for some women at my church. We spent part of one morning talking about the characteristics of a thorn. At the end of our time, I asked, "Are there characteristics of a thorn that we haven't covered? Please tell me if you'd like to add anything."

After class, two women came to tell me similar things. One said, "People assume they know what my thorn is because I had a leg amputated. They think my thorn is the loss of my leg. But those people have no idea. My prosthetic is inconvenient some-times, but it's nothing like the thorn I suffer in private." The second told me, "I have learned that someone else's thorn may not be obvious because most of us keep those things hidden inside."

And so today, as we begin studying the traits of a thorn, maybe you will have some-thing to add along the way. Jot a note in the margin if you do. Maybe you can share what you have with others in your study or post it to me on Facebook®. I want to keep learning how God comes with His sufficient grace in all our different circumstances.

I cannot speak for Paul the apostle. I can only speak for me, not an apostle. But I've come to know many of the barbs of a thorn by now. As we work through these characteristics, maybe you will recognize a similar place of pain in your own life. More importantly, I pray God will give a comfort in your understanding.

Things we MUST tell Angela!

1.

A THORN CANNOT BE REMOVED
BY YOUR OWN POWER.

Paul said, "I pleaded with the Lord three times to take it away from me" (2 Cor. 12:8, HCSB).

Three times Paul asked God to remove his thorn, and three times the thorn remained. I assume that Paul asked God to remove his thorn after he had tried everything he could think of in his own strength.

Before we go one step further, have you asked God to remove your thorn? He does remove thorns, you know. How has God responded to your thorn-removal prayers?

- ❀ I prayed, and God yanked that thorn from me!
- ❀ I prayed for a long, long time, and God finally answered.
- ❀ Same thing as Paul—I keep praying but my thorn remains.
- ❀ Honestly, I haven't ever prayed about it.

I believe if Paul suffered a physical ailment, he sought treatment. If his thorn was a human opponent, I believe he had tried to intervene, negotiate, or run away from the relationship. Honestly, I think Paul probably did everything he thought to do.

For myself, if there were any way to reach down and pull this thing from my life, I would. I have fasted, prayed, sought counsel, screamed, felt sorry for myself, read books, journaled. Anything. Everything. But year after year goes by and I cannot remove this thorn.

Others have tried to remove my thorn. But there is nothing they can say or do. The thorn is so deep. It will not be moved because we are smart or savvy or spiritual. I have come to believe that this is my thorn to bear and yet not mine to remove.

How have you tried to remove your thorn?

What conclusions have you come to about its place in your life?

Maybe, like me, you have spent years proving the truth of this thorn trait: A thorn cannot be removed by your own power. Does that give you any comfort at all, to know that sometimes there is nothing we can do? How do you feel about this aspect of the thorn?

2.

THE ORIGINATOR OF THE THORN IS SATAN.

A lot of people get nervous when you talk about the Devil. Then other people spend way too much time talking about the Devil. I bring him up for a few reasons.

Satan is real.
He is currently at work on this earth.
Paul said that his thorn was
      "a messenger of Satan" (2 Cor. 12:7).

How do you feel when I tell you that the originator of the thorn is Satan?

It's brave to examine the very thing that causes you pain, understanding how you are affected in body, spirit, and mind.

I don't see demons so much, but I believe in them. I also don't think that every bad thing or every inconvenience is the work of a demon. We live in a fallen world, and people make mistakes. Even really good people do dumb things that result in negative consequences. We certainly bring enough heartache on ourselves, but the Bible says Satan is the author of evil. He is the rival of God, and everything he does works against the kingdom of God. He wants people to miss the truth of eternity, and he is the giver of thorns.

What you need to know about Satan as the originator of your thorn is that he has purposed the thorn for evil in your life. He wants to hurt you, discourage you, and tell you lies. Satan is mean, and I hate him. How has Satan used a thorn for evil in your life?

3.
A THORN TORMENTS THE SOUL WITH PAIN AND DOUBT.

Paul wrote that the thorn he suffered was sent by Satan to torment him. Arrrggghhhhhh. I just hate this. Because it's true! The thorn does torment us. It makes me even angrier that Satan is the one jabbing that thing into my heart. But here's what can happen: We can ask ourselves the why questions and then move on to doubt our own worth. We can begin to wonder: *Do I deserve this somehow? Have I caused this pain? Is this a consequence of some mistake I made or sin I committed?*

Even the solidly grounded believer can give in to the pain and begin doubting her worth because of a thorn.

How about you? **What doubts have tormented your heart and mind?**

Know this about God: He may allow a thorn, but Scripture teaches that what Satan means for evil, God can use for good. You need to know that God does not give a thorn as punishment. Because the thorn is from Satan, its purpose is for evil. It's the ongoing, day after day pain that causes your doubts, and the uninformed words of others can fuel even more doubt. Satan wants you to doubt God's love for you. Many days his strategy works.

How has Satan used a thorn to make you doubt God's love?

The deep barbs of a thorn are so painful. I pray that as we talk them through, you find comfort. I have spent years talking through my thorn—sometimes with a safe friend and every day with God. It just helps me to remember what this thing actually is and who God is. I remind you again today that God gave Paul an answer. He gives the same answer to every thorn-bearer today:

His grace is sufficient.

My brave Bible study friend, remember how good God is today. Your thorn is not for punishment. Neither is mine. God promises to turn even what was meant for evil into good (Gen. 50:20). I pray He is doing that in your life even now. I pray that the sweet salve of His grace will wash over your wound, and even if your thorn remains, that its pain would decrease and its presence not overwhelm you.

Let's keep seeking the character of God together. His name is *El Shaddai*. He is enough.

> The brave woman is learning to trust in the God who allows a thorn to pierce His beloved.

THE BARBS OF A THORN

PART TWO

To trust in the sovereignty of God while enduring a thorn is an incredibly brave attitude. I pray that as we study the suffering of thorns this week, God will reveal His character to you. **The only thing that makes me brave is knowing I belong to the One who says:**

I AM able ... to remove your thorn in My time.

I AM sufficient ... while this thorn is yours to bear.

I AM good ... even while you are enduring this pain.

I AM omniscient ... able to see the work happening in your soul.

I AM here ... and you are never alone.

What is God revealing to you about His character?

If you are anything like me, I have to talk things out. I've needed to do this since my earliest remembrance of middle school. I want to think things through. Have the same thoughtful conversation two or three times. Ask the same questions and different questions. Let the truths of a circumstance settle inside of me, and then I talk through the ways I can respond. It's just me.

Talking something through

helps me apply a logical approach, and that helps me feel at peace because I've really sought God and counsel and searched my own heart.

How about you?

Are you a **"talk it through"** girl or a **"think about it privately"** girl?

I've talked through my thorn a thousand times. For some reason, getting a handle on the characteristics of a thorn has helped me. Helped me understand what I'm facing. Helped me think about how I'll respond to the next jab. Helped me trust God more. Helped me to become brave. I hope that as we finish up this day of "barbs," just talking this thing through will help you too. And so, here come the next three characteristics of a thorn.

4.

A THORN WEAVES DISCOURAGEMENT INTO YOUR HEART.

~~~~~~~~~~~~~~~~

I remember the passionate, carefree, live-for-Jesus girl I was pre-thorn. You know the kind of girl. Always talking like I just got home from the most amazing spiritual retreat ever. No discouragement. No negativity. Actually, no real understanding about how sometimes life can just flat-out hurt. I was a spark always looking to get a fire going. Pass it on. Throw the stick of your sin into the campfire and tell the world that Jesus is the answer!

But a thorn, oh my goodness, the thorn can steal your passion and leave you desperately discouraged. The pain leaves you discouraged and questioning. The thorn makes you doubt your calling and can leave you wondering if anything really matters anymore. Paul said Satan sent a thorn to torment him. To torment means to cause severe mental or physical suffering. Severe mental and physical suffering and discouragement go hand in hand. One comes attached to the other.

How would you describe your pre-thorn life?

Some of the modern-day signs of discouragement are:

Sleeplessness
The mind and soul are full of worry, keeping you awake.

Restlessness
Absentmindedness sets in, and weariness results.

Complacency
Unconcern yields loss of interest in food, work, and activities.

Negative thoughts
The mind is consumed with the thorn and its pain.

What other signs of discouragement have you experienced or seen?

Maybe if we remember discouragement is a by-product of the thorn, we can remember God's grace is sufficient for even the deepest discouragement. Our only answer on this journey is God's character and His provision for us. Maybe we can begin battling our discouragement by taking the following actions:

1. Tell God the truth about how discouraged you are. Read Psalm 69:1-3 and see how honest the writer was. You can be that honest with God about your own pain.

2. Give God your discouragement. Read the following verses, and in the margin write all the action verbs.

Proverbs 3:5-6
Philippians 4:6-7
1 Peter 5:7

Look at all the words you wrote. What is God asking you to do today?

3. Ask God for His peace. God loves to transfer His peace to His baby girls. He is the God of peace who sent His Son, the Prince of peace. Look at John 16:33 and see what Jesus said about our discouragement, trouble, and pain.

In **whom** will we find our peace?

What will we have in this world?

Who has overcome every discouragement on our behalf?

5.
THE PIERCING OF A THORN PRODUCES WEAKNESS.

Three times in 2 Corinthians 12 we read that Paul had known great weakness.

Jesus said to Paul, "My power is made perfect in weakness." Then Paul went on to say, "Therefore I will boast all the more gladly about my weaknesses, so that Christ's power may rest on me" (2 Cor. 12:9). Again in verse 10 he said, "That is why, for Christ's sake, I delight in weaknesses, in insults, in hardships, in persecutions, in difficulties. For when I am weak, then I am strong."

What kind of **weakness** has a thorn produced in your life?

Have you been like Paul, boasting in the perfect power of Christ that made him strong? Or have you whined to anyone who would listen about the thorn that makes you weak? I have been a bona fide whiner who is becoming a boaster. How about you?

6.
GOD DECIDES WHEN TO REMOVE A THORN.

As I'm working on this study, this week has been a tough thorn week. Some days the thorn gets pushed, and its barbs dig a little deeper. I can do absolutely nothing but pray. I just finished a thorn interaction, and on the way back to my computer I heard my soul asking God, "How much longer, Lord?" I sat down and looked straight at characteristic 6 above and smiled at how God teaches the teacher.

Paul asked God three times to remove his thorn. I keep proving I am not an apostle, just a girl, because I've asked Him thousands of times to remove mine. But only God can remove a thorn. In His time. In His way. I also believe God leaves the thorn because I still have more left to learn. He seeks a maturity that I have yet to reach.

Believe me, if I could set myself free, I would. I'm sure you would too. But we are both on God's time line with this. Which of these thoughts most closely reflects where you are today?

☐ I'm steaming mad at God about allowing this thorn for me to deal with.

☐ I'm still trying to remove my own thorn in my own power.

☐ I've gone numb to the thorn and to my life.

☐ I am beginning to accept God's authority and His will.

☐ I am learning to boast in my weakness.

For a couple of days we've focused on the pain of our thorns. I hope you haven't fallen into a pit of depression just talking about them. I'm praying that we're getting smarter as we learn to recognize the thorn and all its barbs in our lives. Because we've spent the past two days on this, I'm praying we'll live stronger. **Can I pray for you today?**

Sweet Heavenly Father,
I'm asking You to flood the room where my friend reads these words. Would You fill up her world with Your presence, comfort, and grace? Please let her know that You see the thorn she suffers. You know its pain in her life. You are not far off. You are here.

Keep teaching us about Your sufficiency. You are enough. You make strength from our weakness. You get the glory with our endurance. Oh Lord, make it so for each one of us. Give us new mercy for this day.

Bless all my sisters who suffer a thorn. Lord, bless them. Encourage them. Comfort them. Send someone to love them. And God, according to Your purpose, will You remove every thorn that can be taken away?

So very amen and amen.

> The truly brave are not arrogant. The truly brave are filled with humility over God's grace.

HUMILITY

Last night I went to bed praying for today's lesson. Before I went to sleep, I asked God to show me how to teach this day's study about humility. This morning I woke up from an awful dream. I was in college (the setting of all my nightmares) running to class beside Donald Miller (one of my favorite authors who is much younger than me and couldn't possibly have been my classmate).

I had one high-heel shoe on and one in my hand. My backpack was jammed with who knows what and I was talking a mile a minute. Donald was cool and collected about whatever I was telling him, but I was arrogant. Acting like a know-it-all and embarrassingly haughty. Then I was startled awake with my heart still pounding from the dream.

My first thought was that I was so happy not to be back in college. Then I thought:

Wait a minute. I asked the Lord to teach me about humility. Why did I have that awful dream about being arrogant?

Oh. I get it. That was the me I could have been ... and maybe still could be.

But for the grace of God and the piercing of my thorn, I am absolutely sure I could have become a pious, academic, know-it-all. The truth is that the 20-something years of my thorn have changed me. I am a better person because I carry it every day. I'd like to think I'd be good now without it, but obviously God knows better.

Paul said that he had been given a thorn, "To keep me from becoming conceited" (2 Cor. 12:7). The thorn gave him humility, maybe even a humility he had never thought to desire for himself. Thorns do that. They burst your bubble. Put a limp in your walk. Bring you down to size. Keep you from thinking you're a big shot.

> *"Because of the extravagance of those revelations, and so I wouldn't get a big head, I was given the gift of a handicap to keep me in constant touch with my limitations. Satan's angel did his best to get me down; what he in fact did was push me to my knees. No danger then of walking around high and mighty!"*
>
> 2 CORINTHIANS 12:7, THE MESSAGE

What about you?

Has your thorn produced humility in your life too?

Just a personal thought about humility. I guess as a seminary student I had hoped I could choose humility through obedience to Christ. I would learn about humility from the Scriptures, apply that truth to my life, follow Jesus wholeheartedly, and therefore live as a humble woman. I still think that can happen for some people. But God in His sovereignty has allowed this longer, deeper, wider lesson about humility with my thorn.

So let's look at some of the truths about humility from Scripture.

1. The importance of this virtue comes from the fact that it is found as part of the character of God. **Turn to Psalm 113 and answer a few questions.**

Who is to be praised?

Who is exalted over all the nations?

Who sits enthroned on high?

I bet you get it by now. The psalmist wanted us to see that God is incomparably high and great. And yet look at verse 6.

What does our great and high God do?

He stoops. Our God, who is the great I AM, who is above all things and Lord of all things, humbles Himself to come to His created with love, concern, and mercy.

2. Wherever the quality of humility is found in the Old Testament, it is praised and God frequently pours His blessing on those who possess it. Take a minute to read these three proverbs for a glimpse about how God feels toward the humble.

Proverbs 15:33
Proverbs 18:12
Proverbs 29:23

According to these three verses, what one word sums up the blessing of God for the humble?

3. We find the New Testament uses the same word for *humility* to express a spirit of lowliness that enables God to bring His blessing. In Philippians Paul, our fellow thorn-bearer, taught about the humility of Christ and the humility of his affliction, but I want you to see something in chapter 4:

"I know what it is to be in need, and I know what it is to have plenty. I have learned the secret of being content in any and every situation, whether well fed or hungry, whether living in plenty or in want. I can do everything through him who gives me strength."

PHILIPPIANS 4:12-13

Oh my goodness, Paul was giving us a key here. He taught us that the virtue of humility comes from accepting the humbling experience. Accepting our thorns leads us toward true humility. A condition from without can teach us a corresponding attitude from within.

This is a very big deal! We've all **fussed** about our thorns, **cried, stomped, prayed,** and **yanked at** the thing that gives us so much heartache. But how many of us have learned the secret of contentment in any and every situation?

How about you? Where do you put yourself on this scale of acceptance?

DENIAL

—

—

—

—

COMING TO TERMS

—

—

—

ACCEPTANCE

"In the Bible, the quality called humility is closely connected with affliction, which is sometimes brought upon men by their fellows, and sometimes attributed directly to the purpose of God, but is always calculated to produce humility of spirit."[2] No matter what kind of humbling experience you have or thorn you may suffer, the character-building question is, "Have you allowed it to shape the virtue of humility in your spirit?"

If your answer is "Not yet," what keeps you from receiving the secret of contentment?

Look at the following benefits of humility. According to the Bible, these are some of the blessings God adds to the humble. Look up the corresponding passages as you consider each benefit and your desire for God's blessing.

THOSE WHO HAVE HUMILITY:

are regarded by God . . . . Isaiah 66:2

enjoy the presence of God . . . . Isaiah 57:15

are delivered by God . . . . Job 22:29

are lifted up by God . . . . James 4:10

are exalted by God . . . . Luke 14:11

are the greatest in God's kingdom . . . . . . Matthew 18:4

receive more grace . . . . Proverbs 3:34

are upheld by honor . . . . Proverbs 18:12

Is there a passage above that you need to pray for yourself today? I'll pray the passage from Isaiah 66:2 for myself to show you what I mean.

"Oh Lord, I long to be one whom You esteem. God, teach me how to grow in humility and to keep a contrite spirit. Lord, let me tremble with joy and hunger and reverence for Your Word. Amen." —Writer's paraphrase

Our thorns can teach us a great deal about humility. If we will learn the lesson of Paul, we can receive into our spirits this valued character trait. Our thorns can make us humble. Humility finds its origin in the character of God. God adds blessings to the humble. Acceptance of our circumstances gives us humility. We are to put on this valuable attribute and wear our humility to bring glory to God (see Col. 3:12; Eph. 4:2).

I once wanted to learn about humility from a distance. Keep it academic and yet have it become a part of my character. Turns out that is not how we acquire humility. Many times it comes to us in the thorns. I'm praying for me and for you that each of us is learning to live in the secret of Paul, the secret of contentment and acceptance of what we cannot change. May the humility of our thorns become a beautiful coat to be worn for the glory of God.

I love you, my brave friend.

"Humility is a grateful and spontaneous awareness that life is a gift, and it is manifested as an ungrudging and unhypocritical acknowledgment of absolute dependence upon God."[3]

Humility is not thinking less of yourself; it's thinking of yourself less.

DAY 5

SUFFICIENT GRACE

Each week we're bringing our honest questions to the Scripture and seeking the same destination—knowing the character of God. This week we've spent four days in a passage of Scripture about a thorn. We've talked about our thorns and the pain of their barbs. I'd guess that not one of us bravely received our thorns. Not me, baby; no brave girl here. My thorn has taken every brave cell that might have been part of my DNA and one by one has cut them all away.

How about you?

What has been your bravest thorn moment so far?

What was your most cowardly moment?

I've been insecure and afraid most of the time. God is only making me brave since I learned where to hide. I have learned to hide behind God. He is big, and my thorn is little. He is good. My thorn was sent for evil. He answers my cries with the goodness of who He is. God spoke to Paul hundreds of years ago regarding his thorn, "My grace is sufficient for you, for my power is made perfect in weakness" (2 Cor. 12:9).

With all my heart, I believe God speaks those words to us again today. He will do so, over and over, until we learn how to hide ourselves in the truth of His character. According to this passage, God speaks directly concerning the thorn and promises us—His grace. His sufficiency. His power. His perfection.

You are only responsible to bring yourself and your weakness (your thorn).

You've probably got that part covered. Me too. So let's spend this day looking at God's promises for every thorn-sufferer. In advance, let's thank the Lord that this passage about a thorn doesn't end with the pain. We do have a hope. We have a God who stoops from heaven with His mercy. Not one of us is alone. God has already provided a way for us to endure and even to thrive. Remember, He is *El Shaddai* ... the all-sufficient God.

1. His grace. Grace is God's unmerited favor toward the undeserving and the ill-deserving—God giving sinners (and thorn-bearers) better than they deserve. Grace is the means by which we are saved. It is God's goodness toward us beyond our ability to understand why. In this passage, God promised His grace for our thorns. What does it mean for you to receive the promise of God's grace for your thorn?

God's grace to me means:

In addition to the big picture of grace and a big concept of God's goodness, I believe God gives smaller, everyday graces that minister to us. Heal us. Encourage us.

Some of God's everyday graces for me include …

- 🌼 the times I braced for the thorn to pierce me with a new pain, but God said, "Not today"

- 🌼 when I meet a person I would have never known without my thorn

- 🌼 when just the right word was spoken by just the right person at just the right time

Can you remember a specific everyday grace God gave you for your thorn?

When you receive such beautiful gifts from God, the first thing you want to do is give to someone else what has been given to you. The grace of God is not a secret you keep locked in your soul.

——

Do you need a fresh reminder of God's grace for your thorn?

——

2. His sufficiency. Sufficient means God is enough—not almost enough or barely enough but fully and completely enough. God promises enough grace for us to endure our thorns and to thrive. His sufficiency means that we will make this journey according to His plan and purpose and that His grace will give us endurance and encouragement to strengthen us in our suffering.

How does God show you His grace is enough—maybe not your desired answer—but enough?

How does sufficient grace give you new strength?

3. His power. God is changing our focus so we can see His power in our weakness. Paul was stretched beyond his limits to make him realize that he was dependent on God's power. God wants us to see His power. He wants us to worship Him as master of every circumstance. He wants us to trust that His power is being perfected through us.

I finally gave up and stopped pretending I could muscle up and get through this thorn thing. Exhausted and weary, I finally ran to hide myself inside the power of God. And I testify to you, even though the thorn remains, God's power has been manifest and real. I have seen with my own eyes God's power in my life and ministry. I've seen too much to ever ignore this force of heaven. God is all-powerful, and when He brings His power to your weakness, buckle up. You will see mountains move and hearts of stone made new.

I now realize that I had never really seen the power of God until I was completely dependent on Him from my thorn.

4. His perfection. If God's power is made perfect in our weakness, then maybe we are being taught to view our thorns with new eyes. What if God is asking us to have a new outlook on the very thing that causes us unrelenting heartache so that His glory will be perfected in us and through us?

Do you have a new outlook about your thorn?

If so, what has changed?

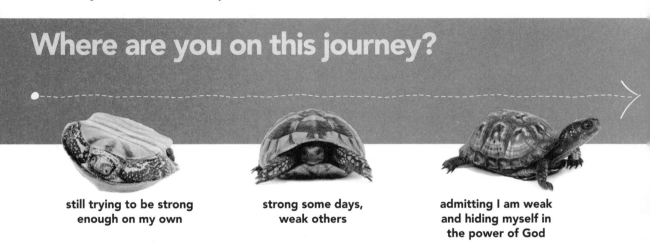

Where are you on this journey?

still trying to be strong enough on my own

strong some days, weak others

admitting I am weak and hiding myself in the power of God

Our world boasts of its strengths and diminishes its weakness.

Paul said he would **boast** of his weakness.

Why do you think he said that?

In what ways are you learning to boast in your weakness?

What if our thorns are a part of God's perfect plan for us?

Can you trust in God's perfect ways even though you bear a thorn?

God said His power is made perfect in our weakness. Maybe the ability to accomplish God's tasks does not rely on our adequacy or even our comfort but in God's ability to perfect His power in our weakness. God is perfect in His character, and that perfect character shines brilliantly through our complete dependence on Him.

As a noun *perfect* means absolute, complete, flawless. That means nothing else to add or to accomplish.

My sweet, dear friend: I imagine this week has been hard for you at times. But I hope it has also been healing. I know it has been for me. This afternoon my thorn remains, and it affects everything and every relationship in my life. It's probably the same for you. I am praying for both of us that God will pour out His sufficient grace on us. I am asking that His grace will be a soothing balm for your wounds. And I pray that His power, all the power of our great and glorious God, will be perfected in our weakness.

May all the thorn girls show off the glory of God today, tomorrow, and forever and ever. Amen.

i am suffering a
thorn

Session 3 Viewer Guide
2 CORINTHIANS 12:7-10, NIV

The Barbs of a Thorn

1. A thorn cannot be removed by _____ _____ power.

2. The originator of the thorn is _____.

3. The thorn torments with _____ and _____.

4. A thorn weaves _____ into your life.

5. The piercing of the thorn produces _____.

6. God decides when to _____ the thorn.

   Verse 7: The thorn was to keep Paul from becoming _____.

   Humility means you are _____ _____ _____ and without pretension.

   El Shaddai means the _____ God.

Note: "Faith is confidence that what God promised or said will come to pass. Sight is the opposite of faith. If you can clearly see how something can be accomplished, more than likely, faith is not required." Henry and Richard Blackaby with Claude King, *Experiencing God: Knowing and Doing the Will of God* (Nashville: LifeWay Press, 2007), 138.

Video sessions are available for download at *www.lifeway.com/women*

WEEK 3

· · · · · · · · · · · · · · · · · ·

i am UN disciplined

When you read the title for this week, I hope your head spoke to your heart, **"Her too?"**

I hope you felt a little comfort in knowing you're not alone. We all, and maybe I should shout-type this, **WE ALL** struggle with areas of undiscipline. Mine may be different than yours, but trust me, this question bounces around in the heart of every woman.

This week let's look forward to the answers God will give. I believe He is going to meet us in our honesty. I think He'll give us encouragement we hadn't expected, and I pray He'll be our guide as we grow, change, and commit to start again for His glory.

So come with me, all you who might be embarrassed to ask of God: "Do You know that I am undisciplined?" Let us receive His goodness and mercy afresh for the journey. Wouldn't it be just like God to make the undisciplined woman brave enough to try again?

I believe that's exactly what He has in mind.

THE STRUGGLE WITHIN

If **I really didn't want to write about an honest question, it was this one.** *Lord, do You know that I'm undisciplined?* Come on, who really wants to bring that up? Who wants to own her lack of discipline? Not me. I figured you didn't either.

OK, honestly,
how do you feel about the topic for this week?

> The brave woman takes ownership of the areas of undiscipline in her life.

Something got hold of me about tackling this idea. Maybe it was a righteous desire to tell the truth. I imagine it was actually the pushing and shoving of the Holy Spirit, but just so you know, I'm going with righteous desire. Finally, I knew the thing I didn't want to talk about was the very thing I had to talk about.

I have written this week more for me than for you. I've written from my sadness and my dogged determination to figure this one out. What keeps so many of us undisciplined in our different areas of struggle? What holds me down? What is it for you?

The bigger idea is that we understand our true source of help. Like me, you may realize a little help is not going to cut it anymore. I need a radical, life-altering, God-sized change. I need a new mind, a new want-to, and a new strength where all the little helps have already failed. Don't shame me or beat me up with more guilt; I've done enough of that already. I need the God of heaven to make some old parts of me new. A Holy Spirit change—that's what I'm seeking from the Lord this week.

God promises He can change us. I believe that with all of my heart, so I'm leading the charge toward this truth. Loud and bold. Humbled and honest. God can change every lack of discipline in our lives and be the strength we have not known.

I guess there's only one way to start this. 'Fess up. I'll go first to take the edge off. Hear me: What I'm getting ready to do is by no means an exhaustive list. What I promise to do is add to my list this week as the Lord brings things up. I want to get it all on the table. Like I said, I feel like I'm writing for me first on this, so I have been undisciplined with my:

eating habits

exercise

schedule

studying

commitment to family and friends

physical health (vitamins, check-ups, etc.)

letter writing, especially thank-you notes

follow through giving little gifts

finishing things I really intend to do

Here's the part where I invite you to be honest with your struggles. Before you do, I want to acknowledge that some of you are wrestling with a lack of discipline in areas such as addictions, relationships, and finances. These battles are many days fierce and consuming. Maybe this is the page where you answer on a separate sheet of paper. No one else needs to see where you struggle with a lack of discipline. If you're in a small group, don't feel pressured to share anything here. We all feel guilty enough

without the blank stares of people we love who don't share the same issues. The point is to at least be honest with God.

A few weeks ago I said to my friend, "If I could find the switch for self-discipline, we could rescue the world." Nodding in agreement, she replied, "Call me when you have it." Obviously, there's no switch, and I think that's the point with God. Greater discipline is about maturity, and for most of us it's a journey of spiritual maturity that takes us to God.

Here is the space for your honest list:

Maybe the next time someone shares a struggle, I can resist the temptation to trump her struggle with a bigger one I've heard about. I will bite my tongue before I give her three easy ways to overcome. I will listen with great empathy and ask if I can walk with her toward finding an answer. Then I can pray with consistency and meaning.

ONE HONEST MAN

Maybe it will help you to know we are not alone in wanting to do better. I'm so grateful the Bible gives us real stories of struggle so I can be assured this is not just some Busy Mom Syndrome. Turn with me to the Book of Romans. We return again to honest Paul and his honest admission: "I do not understand what I do. For what I want to do I do not do, but what I hate I do. ... For I have the desire to do what is good, but I cannot carry it out. For what I do is not the good I want to do; no, the evil I do not want to do—this I keep on doing. ... So I find this law at work: When I want to do good, evil is right there with me. For in my inner being I delight in God's law; but I see another law at work in the members of my body, waging war against the law of my mind and making me a prisoner of the law of sin at work within my members" (Rom. 7:15,18-19,21-23).

Paul said that he knew what he longed to do and how he longed to live, but inside of him a war raged—good against evil. Do you feel that same kind of war inside of you?

What triggers have you identified that set off the war inside you again?

The Bible calls this war the flesh against the Spirit. The good we want to do to improve ourselves battles the pull of our flesh (the old nature) that pulls at us to distract us from what is right. Look at what Paul wrote to the Galatians: "The sinful nature desires what is contrary to the Spirit, and the Spirit what is contrary to the sinful nature. They are in conflict with each other, so that you do not do what you want" (Gal. 5:17).

We desire greater discipline in an area and then choose the opposite. The battle is real, and it is spiritual. The only way to change a spiritual battle is to fight in the Spirit. If we could will ourselves into an answer, we would have already done that. This battle that goes on inside of us is a battle that can only be won by God.

I am currently watching someone I love be changed before my eyes. The Spirit of God is changing her character, her habits, and her countenance. Nobody can ever tell me God is not big enough for the hardest hearts. I have seen Him with my own eyes. He is big enough for your struggles and for mine.

In Romans 7 Paul gave us all hope. "Who will rescue me [feel free to insert your name here] from this body of death?" The death Paul referred to is his personal struggle in not doing the good he desired. "Thanks be to God—through Jesus Christ our Lord!" (Rom. 7:24-25).

Paul said that **our only rescue from the war in our flesh comes from God through Jesus Christ. Do you know that Jesus is our answer? Because He is! Breathe a thank-You prayer to God. No matter how many areas of undiscipline you wrote on your list earlier, Jesus is the answer. No matter how many years you have struggled, Jesus is the answer. No matter how discouraged you may be, my friend, Jesus is our answer.**

THE SPIRIT HELPS US

Yesterday I told you I am witnessing a bona fide miracle in someone I love. Actually, I'm not the only one. Everyone who knows this person is flabbergasted by the change. Mind you, this is not just a little improvement; she is radically different. Everything is jaw-droppingly improved. Smile. Attitude. Works. Service. Heart. Mind. Generosity. If you asked her what's going on, she would tell you, "I am being changed by Jesus." One day this person said to me, "It's like I've been asleep and now I'm waking up!" Can you imagine that?

I'm thrilled for everything happening with my friend. I love knowing she has a new hope and future, but I'm sure God played this real-life movie out in front of me to show what He can do in my life and in yours. He is the God of our impossible. He breaks old habits and frees prisoners of addiction from their chains. No one but God could have changed the one I love.

Do you love someone for whom change seems impossible? Ask the God of the impossible to come to that person's rescue. Have you given up on yourself? Has change been too hard and disappointing? Maybe you're the one who needs a bona fide miracle. I think it's perfectly right to ask God for your own personal miracle here too.

Let's get back to Paul in the Book of Romans. He said that we have two choices. We can be controlled by the sinful nature that is still inside of us, or we can live according to the guidance of the Holy Spirit. "Those who live according to the sinful nature have their minds set on what that nature desires; but those who live in accordance with the Spirit have their minds set on what the Spirit desires. The mind of the sinful man is death, but the mind controlled by the Spirit is life and peace" (Rom. 8:5-6).

The one I love has chosen to surrender to the living, life-giving Spirit of God. I think that's how we all are changed. Both the little areas and the big ones demand a giving-up, a sacrifice, a renouncing. We throw in the towel to the old ways our flesh controls us, and we turn toward the strength of the Spirit to make us who the Lord longs for us to be.

Maybe you have given up trying. Given up on your plan. Or given up on your steps toward recovery. That is not the giving up we're talking about.

Paul said we have to give up the control of our desires. We have to give control to the Spirit and relinquish the control of our flesh.

> **The brave woman knows determination will not be enough and asks the Holy Spirit to change her very nature.**

A lightweight example would be if chocolate chip cookies control you and you long for them more than you long to be healthy. Instead of following a plan about counting cookies, the power will come when we give up the control the cookie has in our minds. I am bigger than a cookie. You are bigger than a cookie. But for many of us, the cookie is winning. We can no longer live according to the cookie. We must live in accordance with what the Spirit desires. I would imagine the Spirit desires we enjoy a couple of cookies and not allow ourselves to be controlled by dough and chips.

Not one of us wants to be controlled by

ALCOHOL IN A BOTTLE

THE SOFA IN FRONT OF THE TELEVISION

A CARTON OF ICE CREAM IN THE FREEZER

HANGERS OF NEW CLOTHES IN A DEPARTMENT STORE

THE HABIT OF TRUSTING PEOPLE WHO HURT US

What are some things that control the people you care for?

What about you?
Does something seem to have a hold over you?

A Little Theology Lesson

We are filled with the Holy Spirit, so why can't a Christian woman be completely disciplined all the time?

When one decides to follow Christ and comes to be "in the Spirit," she is no longer in the flesh, but the flesh is still in her. In fact, a struggle between the flesh and the Spirit remains in the believer. Writing to people who are "in the Spirit," Paul said, "For the sinful nature desires what is contrary to the Spirit, and the Spirit what is contrary to the sinful nature. They are in conflict with each other, so that you do not do what you want" (Gal. 5:17). Because the Christian life is the battleground of these two opposing principles, it is impossible to be the perfect person that one would wish to be.

69

I know you already realize this, but

God is bigger.

Bigger than whatever you've given control. He is able to subdue our desires, change our nature, and take control of our compulsions. Many of us struggle with lack of discipline because we have given control to something else.

We are undisciplined with food because we have given in to our flesh.

We are undisciplined with money and again choose the desires of our flesh.

We are undisciplined with our words—you got it—choosing the flesh instead.

The control of the flesh and the struggle within is our weakness.

Paul continued: "In the same way the Spirit also joins to help in our weakness, because we do not know what to pray for as we should, but the Spirit Himself intercedes for us with unspoken groanings. And He who searches the hearts knows the Spirit's mind-set, because He intercedes for the saints according to the will of God." (Rom. 8:26-27, HCSB).

Do you hear this? I love it. Paul said it's OK for us not to know what to pray. That's the job of the Holy Spirit. We bring our weakness to Him, and He knows how to pray. Hallelujah! So many times I don't have any idea what to do, and this passage is so comforting to me. I just bring my weakness to God, and the Spirit prays for me in accordance with His will. According to this passage, we can pray things like this:

Lord, I am weak. Chips and salsa have a ridiculous control over me. And now the Spirit is going to pray for me because I don't know what to do.

Lord, I am attracted to bad people. They hurt me and wound me. And now the Spirit is going to pray for me because I don't know what to do.

Lord, I hurt myself with drugs and sexual activity. And now the Spirit is going to pray for me because I don't know what to do.

Do you see the very real application of this verse in your life? The Spirit helps you in your weakness. He prays when you don't know how to pray.

For what weakness do you need the Spirit to pray today?

God knows that we are undisciplined. According to His Word, He has made a way for us. He has sent His Spirit to intercede for us when we don't know what to pray. He has given us a Savior who saves and gives grace to the undisciplined. Through that same Son, Jesus, God offers us strength to become the women we thought we never could be.

The one I love is changing before my eyes, and it's all because of Jesus. I am claiming that same power in my life and in yours. Press into Him, dear one. He has hope for you and me.

LIVING ON FIRE

DAY 3

My son William was invited to play for a soccer team here in North Carolina that is coached by collegiate soccer coaches. When you're 14, being coached by collegiate coaches is a big deal. My little lanky pumpkin eats, sleeps, and dreams soccer. He wears a soccer jersey almost every day, mostly gets in trouble for juggling a soccer ball in the kitchen, and wears us out about soccer trivia from all over the world. I wish some soccer mom would write *Being a Soccer Mom for Dummies* because I desperately need a manual to keep up with this kid.

When William is on the soccer field and we see him connect all his skill and energy to play like a crazy man, we yell to him, "You're on firrrah!" I used to yell, "Way to go, Peanut!" but he's convinced me that "Peanut" is not very motivating. Evidently neither is blowing the horn and waving madly while I'm turning into the fields to pick him up. But when Peanut has his soccer groove on, both his body and mind are fully engaged. I watch him do crazy tricks with his feet, and I am amazed that this child was born from such a clumsy woman. Truly a testimony to God. Maybe the best part is when William is playing "on firrrah," he's having the time of his life.

When I watch William, I am incredibly inspired. Thankfully, I have no aspirations about soccer in my mid-40s, but I am inspired by his passion. I look at him and think to myself, *I want to live like that.* Having the time of my life. Fully engaged. Learning to listen to the prompting of the Holy Spirit, and then, the biggie, obeying God with all of my heart.

> To decide that it's time to become the woman you have always longed to be is incredibly brave.

Who inspires you

to live more passionately?

The past two days we have looked at the Book of Romans and Paul's honest admissions about his own struggles. If we wrote one of those passages for ourselves, maybe it would read a little like this: I do not understand what I do. I want to be a disciplined woman, but I do not consistently pursue discipline. I hate what I do ... for I have the desire to do what is disciplined, but I cannot carry it out. For what I do is not the discipline I want to do; no, the evil I do not want to do—this I keep on doing.

Paul went on to tell us that this war inside of us is a battle between our flesh and the Spirit. We win the battle every time we give up the desires of the flesh, like wanting to sit on the sofa this afternoon, and choose to obey the Spirit, who has been reminding us to take a walk since this morning.

Maybe today you are more aware of the battle within and you can name some of your struggles with regard to discipline. Think of a few of the things going on inside of you. **I'll start:**

THE FLESH vs. THE SPIRIT

I am tempted to nap this afternoon even though I had plenty of rest last night.

Keeps telling me I am strong enough to forgo the nap and finish on schedule today.

THE FLESH vs. THE SPIRIT

All right, your turn!

Now hear me: Some days I really need a nap, and I think naps are OK with God. But if I don't need a nap and the Spirit of God is telling me what to do instead, I am called to obey. That, as you know, is the battle, and that battlefield is where we make choices about becoming more mature followers of Christ or not.

TRAINING REQUIRED

Paul marked out the next piece of this journey toward a disciplined life.

"Don't you know that the runners in a stadium all race, but only one receives the prize? Run in such a way to win the prize. Now everyone who competes exercises self-control in everything. However, they do it to receive a crown that will fade away, but we a crown that will never fade away. Therefore I do not run like one who runs aimlessly or box like one beating the air. Instead, I discipline my body and bring it under strict control, so that after preaching to others, I myself will not be disqualified" (1 Cor. 9:24-27, HCSB).

Paul was passing his notes to us. You remember he faced the same struggles we encounter. He is the same man who wanted one thing and then chose another.

But here, Paul gave us a lesson he fought hard to learn. Becoming a more disciplined woman will require training. A process. Becoming self-disciplined and controlled takes commitment, sacrifice, and focus. Training is the picture Paul drew for us. Just like a runner trains to win a prize, you and I will have to train to conquer the areas of undiscipline we still face.

HOLY DEPENDENCE

Just a thought . . .

What if on this earth we will never be completely disciplined in every area of our lives at the same time? And what if that's on purpose? A design element. A Creator component. An intentional decision by our God so that a holy dependence is required for us to mature toward each new place of discipline.

Maybe God allows my lack of discipline because it keeps me running to Him. His strength is the source by which I will grow into greater discipline. He makes me able to take the next brave step. Maybe if I woke up tomorrow completely disciplined, perfected even, I would think more about myself and my great accomplishment and less about God and how much I need Him.

I do not speak for God, and the Scriptures do not elaborate here, but what if a perfectly disciplined life was never God's intent? What if He intended holy dependence for life-long growth toward Himself?

One of my friends tweeted a few days ago: "I just finished running a 5k on my treadmill. Yep folks, that's 3.2 miles. I remember the day, not so long ago, that I couldn't run for 3.2 minutes."

My friend didn't just plug in her treadmill and run a 5k. She had to train her body to last a few more minutes every day. Her journey from no discipline to greater discipline has come by training and focus and, I'm sure, a few tears along the way.

SELF-DISCIPLINE

—

the ability to regulate one's conduct by principle and sound judgment rather than by impulse, desire, or social custom

Training yourself to be disciplined is probably not a new idea to you, but I am praying that these fresh reminders from Scripture are beginning to relight the fires of desire inside your heart. What would a fresh commitment to training look like for you?

Maybe you want a disciplined prayer life and you could just bend to your knees and start prayer training right now.

For some of you, a fresh commitment might mean driving to a rehab and signing yourself in this afternoon.

For some, maybe it means going to your closet and lacing up your running shoes.

List three tangible ways you could begin training that will lead to discipline:

1.

2.

3.

I wish I were sitting across from you right now. Maybe you need encouragement, and I would totally be your biggest cheerleader. Maybe you can hear my enthusiasm in the words I write to you ... We can do this! I know we can. We can become more disciplined because God knows our need and has met our need through the gift of the Holy Spirit. Every woman who follows Jesus Christ has God's Spirit living inside of her. The power is here. Did you know that? The power to live a disciplined life is already inside of you.

I believe we can be trained to give up the desires of our flesh and instead learn to choose the leading of the Spirit. According to the whole context of Scripture, not one of us is too far gone for God to reach, to change, and to grow!

So pray with me as we wrap up:

God, make me a disciplined woman. I want all of the blessings that come from choosing to follow the Spirit. I want to live on fire! For Your glory and for Your name. Oh Lord, train me. Teach me. Remind me. Nudge me. Rebuke me. I know You haven't given up on me, but Lord, help me not to give up on myself.
I love You and I need You,
amen.

I AM

I AM Father.
The God who is our Father

I AM *El.*
The strong one

I AM the Rock of Ages.
God in His strength and permanency

A WORD TO THE LAZY

Lazy women decide living a brave life is too hard. Their lives are marked by struggle, emptiness, and a lack of power.

When I plan each of the weeks of our Bible study, I make a new file for that week, create and title all the new day's documents, then loosely lay my topic outline across the days. Of course, everything always changes when I actually begin writing the study, but at least the outline keeps me headed in the right direction without too many rabbit trails. You don't have to worry though, because if I rabbit trail anyway, my editor will come along to shoo away the rabbits and herd us all back into line.

Today I opened the document for day 4 and read my forgotten title for today, "A Word to the Lazy," and the first thing I thought was, *Oh no.* Maybe you opened your study today and thought the same thing: *A word to the lazy. Do we really have to? I have only read five words, and I'm convicted already.*

What makes us feel convicted by just reading the word *lazy?*

I know the title may not have drawn you in, but I really think we ought to spend a day here—thinking about lazy, studying about lazy, and praying about lazy. All this should be done without any of us becoming lazier. Are you in? I could worry that the lazy people just turned the page, but I'm stopping myself from thinking like that.

WORDS FROM THE WORD

The Bible has a lot to say about sluggards, lazy people, and fools. I am pretty sure we are not one of those people, yet we all have to be on guard that we don't let any of their traits ever have a place in our lives. It turns out that the fruit of an undisciplined life looks a lot like the life of the lazy. Solomon said many convicting things about such a life in the Book of Proverbs:

> "A little sleep,
> a little slumber,
> a little folding of the
> hands to rest—
> and poverty will come
> on you like a bandit
> and scarcity like an
> armed man."
>
> PROVERBS 6:10-11

> "Like a city whose walls are broken down is a man who lacks self-control."
>
> PROVERBS 25:28

> "As a door turns on its hinges, so a sluggard turns on his bed."
>
> PROVERBS 26:14

> "The sluggard buries his hand in the dish; he is too lazy to bring it back to his mouth."
>
> PROVERBS 26:15

Maybe you just read these passages and said to yourself, *Whew, I am not a sluggard.* Thankfully, most of us are not, even though I do know a few. But probably in truth, some areas in each of our lives have slug potential. We must be aware of the slug potential.

You know what I'm going to ask next, so you might as well be honest with yourself—

In which areas do you have a little slug potential?

1.

2.

3.

The thing about slug potential is that when we allow ourselves to indulge, we also set ourselves up for the consequences. My recent slug potential just rewarded me with 25 extra pounds. Also known as the happy pounds that began coming onto my body the first day of my happy honeymoon, they are 25 unwanted pounds, nonetheless. One of the consequences of my slugness is that I can't wear any of the clothes hanging in my closet. And really, it feels like sin to have nice things that the slug can no longer button around her waist. Another consequence of my choosing is that I became increasingly self-conscious. Really not what I want to happen when my whole life mission statement is about taking my eyes off of myself and loving others to God.

Consequences. Ugh.

Perhaps Solomon referenced the sluggard and lazy so often because its path leads to a dead end. The woman who wants to live on fire will not make sluggard choices and suffer their consequences. So let's commit today to push away from our slug potential and turn toward greater discipline.

Small steps.

We can do this.

Have you suffered your own set of slug consequences? If so, what are they?

In his book *The Pillars of Christian Character*,[2] John MacArthur suggests some

ways to begin:

1 Start with small things.

Clean your room or clean out your pantry. Make one phone call you've been putting off. Buy yourself some good sneakers.

What one small thing will you start with?

2 Get yourself organized.

Your closet. Your desk. Your calendar.

What needs a little organization in your life?
I'm personally thinking about my hall closet, with several more ideas close behind.

3 Don't constantly seek to be entertained.

Truth is, some days discipline is just plain hard work. It's not all going be fun and games. I know that in my head. Sometimes I also have to accept it in my heart.

4 Be on time.

This is not usually my issue. My daddy trained us all to arrive early and drive around the block until time to go in. But some girls reading these words need a fresh commitment to this one. The older I get, the more I enjoy the sanity that comes with getting up early. Maybe you'd like your day better if you started a few minutes before others in your house. That early time gives me a few moments of composure before the pandemonium begins.

5 Keep your word.

Matthew 5:37 says, "Simply let your 'Yes' be 'Yes,' and your 'No,' 'No'; anything beyond this comes from the evil one." Seems like enough said about that serious command.

6

Do the most difficult tasks first.

Go ahead and do the thing you feel most insecure about. Make the phone call you're scared to make. Pay the bill you are dreading to pay. What task do you have in mind right now?

7

Finish what you start.

Maybe the bigger idea is that we start only what God has called us to start.

8

Accept correction.

Solomon wrote: "He whose ear listens to the life-giving reproof will dwell among the wise. He who neglects discipline despises himself, but he who listens to reproof acquires understanding" (Prov. 15:31-32, NASB).

It's interesting that I've read several self-help books while writing about the lack of discipline. Many therapists echo this biblical truth. They say people engage in obsessive (undisciplined) behaviors (such as eating, shopping, spending, you name it) because they don't like themselves. Accepting correction is one of the first steps we need to take toward understanding ourselves, recognizing how we got where we are, and learning to love the person God created us to be.

Tom Landry said, "The job of a football coach is to make men do what they don't want to do, in order to achieve what they've always wanted to be."[3]

None of us wants a football coach yelling while we do one hundred push-ups. But I do want that part about achieving what I've always wanted to be. I'm praying we both learn the art of doing some hard things to achieve God's great things for our lives.

9

Practice self-denial.

We talked about this yesterday. Training ourselves to become disciplined may mean choosing one hot Krispy Kreme® doughnut instead of six or walking to the mailbox instead of driving by.

What one step will you take today toward self-denial?

10

Welcome responsibility.

We cross the line of responsibility when we finally decide we want some things that matter in life. We decide to grow up. Accept where we are. Make a plan to live differently and then work toward our goals. When you welcome responsibility, you decide to stop blaming your past, your family, and your own dumb choices.

Hello responsibility! I finally realize how you are the only one who can make me grow.

OK, my friends, feeling not lazy yet? I sure do. My Ten Little Steps are great ways to begin shaking off my slug potential.

This girl wants to LIVE ON FIRRRAH!

HE IS MY STRENGTH

This morning I am tired. Not sure exactly why, but I'm tired. I tried to go back to sleep, but my head wouldn't let me. So I got up tired and let the dogs outside all sluggy-like. Then I stood in the kitchen and mixed up my miracle-energy vitamins to drink, all the while saying to the Lord, *I am still the woman who wants to live on fire. But I really need You to come and make a new fire inside of me today.*

Alongside the battle of Spirit against flesh inside each of us lies the reality of being a human on this earth. Just when we thought we'd surrendered our slug potential, we wake up one morning tired ... and sluggish. Or we've worked on a determined heart only to have the words of a friend come and wound us with their discouragement. We live on a planet that is fallen and full of sin. Our bodies run out and break down. Our hearts will one day be strong and the next day weak. One moment sure and the next moment fickle.

Since we deal with all these reasons we so desperately need God, I think it's incredibly brave to ask God, "Do You know that I am undisciplined?" because in these weary bodies, with this inner struggle that rages, we will never become what we desire until we take our weakness to the only One who can make us strong.

The Lord responds with His thunderous, heavenly voice, "I am your strength." Thank goodness. This new morning when I desperately need new mercy, my God—who never sleeps, my God who never fails, my God who is the same yesterday, today, and tomorrow—is my strength and yours.

My hormones can sneak up and zap me of energy and strength. How about you? What reminds you how human you are and how inconsistent your strength can be?

I used to be frustrated with myself because I couldn't force my body or mind to respond consistently the way I wanted. I am learning this is what it means to serve God from inside a human vessel. Today that means I'll probably need a nap, and that's OK. Tired girls can take a nap.

How about you?
How have you learned to deal with your very real weakness?

Especially on days like this I am reminded to be grateful. I'm so thankful I have a Savior. I'm thankful God sent His Son to rescue me. Today I am sure I could never rescue myself. Not only did God send His Son but He also sent the Holy Spirit to live inside of us. Through the Holy Spirit God gives us His strength to battle our weakness. The Holy Spirit is powerful enough to overcome every lazy streak, procrastination, and distraction. I believe the Holy Spirit gives strength to weary bodies and discouraged hearts.

Given my own lack of energy this morning, I'm sure I could have just lingered over my coffee instead of working. But I felt like the Holy Spirit said, *Sit at your computer, and let Me be the strength you don't have.*

Do you realize that God wants to give His strength to you too? He works through weary women all the time. He uses the lazy, the disorganized, and the procrastinators.

In what area do you most need Him to make you strong today?

The victory over our lack of discipline will be won when we realize this one thing: We must maintain an intimate, consistent dependence on the Spirit of God inside us.

He is able. We are not. He is strong. We are undisciplined. He is consistent. We are wishy-washy.

No matter how weak you are or how undisciplined you have been, dependence on Him changes everything. The more you train yourself to be dependent on the Spirit of God, the more He bears His fruit in your life. Look at Galatians 5:22-26 in your Bible.

How exciting is this? The Holy Spirit produces in us the very things we could never buy for ourselves. According to verses 22-23, what does a dependence on the Spirit produce in your life?

The brave woman brings her need of discipline to God and asks Him to give what she does not possess.

Tell me, which aspect of the fruit is the very thing you need to move from undisciplined toward greater discipline?

> The Message paraphrase describes self-control as the ability to "marshal and direct our energies wisely."

What six ideas can you think of for everyday Jesus girls like you and me to keep in step with the Holy Spirit?

1.
2.
3.
4.
5.
6.

According to Galatians 5:25,
what action
is required of us?

We are to keep in step with the Holy Spirit. Follow Him. Learn to be dependent on Him. The Message says: "Since this is the kind of life we have chosen, the life of the Spirit, let us make sure that we do not just hold it as an idea in our heads or a sentiment in our hearts, but work out its implications in every detail of our lives" (Gal. 5:25).

Did you get that? Following the Spirit is not an idea or a sentiment. This is how we change from women who know a lot about what to do into women who are doing what we ought. To become a disciplined woman means I choose to obey the Spirit. God gives His strength through the Spirit, and we must keep in step with the Spirit to have His strength.

The Lord knows our needs, weaknesses, and propensity toward a lack of discipline. But He has made a way: When we obey the Spirit, God's strength is set free inside of us.

The next time you recognize the struggle of flesh against spirit, stop and listen for God. Then obey as the Spirit of God leads you, and watch what happens. Every time, and I mean every time, God will add a strength because of your obedience.

We are the women who want to live on fire for God. God brings the fire when we choose to obey the Spirit. Every day I personally ask God for two things:

1. Teach me how to share the gospel.
2. Teach me how to walk in complete dependence.

I pray that God has shown you what He desires for you. I pray that you see how the lack of discipline can be changed into strength. I pray that you see God today—His compassion for you, His new day to start again, and His powerful strength to make you able.

Keep in step with the Spirit, my friend.

The goal is to know God's discipline for _____.

"I do not understand what I do. For what I want to do _____ _____ _____ do, but what I hate I do" (Rom. 7:15).

Paul knows how he longs to live, but inside of him there is a _____ waging.

We must learn to live _____ by the Spirit.

How do we learn to live according to the Spirit?

1. Go into _____, learning to obey. Replace the high of _____ with the high of _____.

2. Stay _____ to the Spirit of God.

3. Recognize the ongoing process of _____.

4. The hinge: You and I will have to _____ as the Spirit leads.

i am
UNdisciplined
Session 4 | *Viewer Guide*
ROMANS 7:15

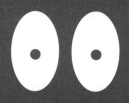

WEEK 4

· ·

i am trembling inside

A couple of weeks ago I drove my husband Scott to the dermatologist's office for a little outpatient surgery. Thankfully, although Scott was left with about 30 stitches on his abdomen and leg, the pathology reports all came back clear.

Scott worked all morning, and he ran by the house to get me so we could go together. We chatted all the way there about work and family. He was seemingly as cool as a cucumber without a mention of worry about his procedure. When the nurse came into the examination room, she walked us through the recovery instructions and began to prep Scott. One of the first things she did was take his blood pressure. I watched his numbers register on the monitor, and they were high. I said to the nurse, "His blood pressure is high."

She looked over and said, "You're right."

"Are you anxious, Mr. Pharr?"

"Maybe a bit," he sheepishly answered.

That whole time I thought my husband was amazingly immune from "a little surgery" anxiety. But his body gave him away. He was trembling on the inside. Unseen by me but known all along by God.

This week we're asking the Lord, "Do You know I'm trembling inside?" The past few days I've tried to pay attention to my fears. I'll be going along fine and a phone call or an e-mail can cause a fear reaction in me. I can feel anxious. A little agitated. Distracted. Nervous in my mind. Then of course the bigger fears leave us paralyzed with anxiety and worry.

From the circle of my fears, I have many times stood paralyzed in the middle when God was calling me to the edge. I have settled for safe even though God called, "Jump into My arms; I have you!" I have allowed mediocre when I knew God wanted excellence.

Maybe you too have let your fears teach you how to live with hesitance and fear. Maybe you've settled for less because fear kept you from trying. Maybe even today you are trembling on the inside with a very real concern or problem.

If fear has been your enemy, I am praying that this week God will be your answer. He is, hallelujah, the God of all comfort.

I pray that this week God will wrap His arms around the trembling and make us brave.

LIVING ALONGSIDE TROUBLE

Last year I was called back to my gynecologist for possible cervical cancer. I remember sitting across from the doctor in his office, smiling politely as he reviewed my tests, and feeling absolutely nothing. Numb. After a while of sitting there in silence, I realized he was talking to me. I took my numb self down the hall to check out, walked through the lobby with my next appointment reminders, and just didn't feel a thing.

In my car I began to feel an old feeling I've known before. I lived that feeling for several years through my separation and divorce. I felt it the day Daddy called to tell me Mama had ovarian cancer. I was swallowed up by it the day my sister drowned.

In the car outside my doctor's office, that sick feeling of fear poured itself into me. My hand holding the papers began to shake. The car keys shook in my fingers. I could barely get the car into reverse with my foot quivering on the brake. The fear was coming, and it made everything inside of me tremble and shake.

Maybe you've heard something that left you frozen and dazed. A test result that indicated cancer. The 401(k) statement that your husband deciphered aloud. A layoff notice read grimly to your entire department. Or the text from a child to tell you he didn't mean to, he is sorry, but he has been arrested. Such news takes your breath away and numbs your soul with dread.

FEAR

Have you ever known the kind of fear that made you tremble on the inside and then worked its way out to make you tremble on the outside? If so, describe that time.

How are the fears of this journey coming at you today?

Maybe you're standing now at the edge of bad news wondering, *How did something so big just sneak into my life?* And maybe you are asking God, "Do You know that I'm trembling inside?"

A series of procedures have now gotten my pathology results back in a normal range, but I'm sure you know life just keeps coming with its little and big fears all along the journey. Some things bring me a surprise fear—like my test results. Other things happen that can ignite an inner fear—like watching the nightly news, having a difficult conversation with a friend, or imagining harm coming to one of my children.

DANGER
STRONG
CURRENT

I'm sure you already know this, but no one gets a free pass in this world. No immunity idols exist to help us become survivors. Cancer, catastrophes, and awful consequences exist because we live in a fallen world. Evil is present. Sin is inside of us and all around us. Not one of Jesus' disciples escaped this lifetime without suffering. They didn't model an insulated life for us. Jesus reminded His disciples, and He reminds us today, "In this world you will have trouble" (John 16:33).

We are called to live alongside trouble—the kind of trouble that causes fear, worry, and trembling on the inside. The Son of God suffered an unimaginable death, even though He lived a flawless life. Who am I to think that somehow I just might skip past adversity? It will not happen for me or for you.

In this world trouble is certain, but we also have the promise of Jesus as He concluded His upper-room message to the disciples:

"I have told you these things, so that in me you may have peace. In this world you will have trouble. But take heart!
I have overcome the world."

JOHN 16:33

You may want to spend some time reading Jesus' entire discourse in John 13–16. Jesus spent three chapters preparing His disciples to live without His physical presence and to be dependent on the indwelling of the promised Holy Spirit.

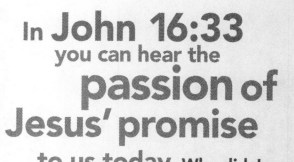

In **John 16:33** you can hear the **passion of Jesus' promise** to us today. **Why did Jesus give His disciples this message?**

**What do we have
IN CHRIST?**

**Notice the
contrast between
"in me" and
"in this world."**

**What do we have
IN THIS WORLD?**

Jesus encouraged us to "Be of good cheer" (John 16:33, KJV). The rationale of His encouragement is based on His promise. What is the promise for those who are in Christ?

Before we zoom past this central teaching, I want to take a minute for you if you're still struggling with where you are with God. One idea about following Jesus sounds very old-fashioned, but I love the word so much that I want us to talk about it.

You've probably heard people say that when you make a decision to be a Christ follower, you are saved. I love that. We are saved. According to this passage, we are saved from being swallowed up by this world's trouble. The rest of Scripture testifies that because of Jesus, we are saved from suffering the eternal penalty of our sins.

The Greek word for "be of good cheer" is *therasite*. It means "Not only be of good comfort, but be of good courage; have a good heart on it, all shall be well."[1] I love that part about "be of good courage." Sounds like those who are in Christ are being made brave.

What does it mean for you to "be of good cheer" even though you may be living alongside trouble and trembling on the inside?

God promises the victory of overcoming to those who are in Christ. In John 15:4, Jesus said, "Abide in me, and I in you" (KJV). To be in Christ means that we are branches of the Living Vine and that apart from Him we are nothing and can do nothing. We have no life in ourselves; our lives now come from Christ.

What does **being saved** mean to you?

Never was a CONQUEROR in this world like Jesus. He conquered Satan.
He conquered sin.
He conquered the cross and the grave.

"We are more than conquerors through him who loved us."
Romans 8:37

Our Conqueror is the only One who can deliver us from our fears. He is the only One who will give us victory over what makes us tremble inside. Christ has overcome the world and all the troubles in this world. For all of us who are in Christ, we have nothing left to do but pursue the victory.

Whatever fears this day has brought to you, whatever makes you tremble inside, I want you to know that God in His great love poured out His Son Jesus as the first wave of His divine comfort for us.

All who are in Christ have been saved.
Can you close your eyes and let that great truth give renewed comfort to your soul?
I want to pray for you as we close.

Oh Jesus, thank You for saving me. Sometimes I forget that I am already saved. I forget where to take my fears. I forget that the victory over this world is already won. So thank You for never changing. Thank You for loving me. Thank You for the peace that comes from trusting You more. Today I want to "be of good cheer" because I remember I am in You. You are my conqueror. You are my hope. You are my peace. Oh hallelujah, I am saved. Amen and amen.

THE GOD OF ALL COMFORT

I trust God completely. But honestly, just like you, at times I have to remind myself what I believe and to whom I belong. Most importantly, I need to remember who God is. He is I AM. He is Creator, Redeemer, Comforter, and Healer. But I am just a human, so when a fear sometimes comes to me, my human anxiety will kick in, and the trembling inside begins. I feel that trouble for all the same reasons you do:

- every time Mama has a doctor's visit to check for cancer
- when a huge bill that I had no idea was due comes in the mail
- when I'm going into a meeting that could be hard or disappointing
- when my children call with that catch in their voices

In our fears and frustration, we can tremble with apprehension and sadness. But today I want to tell you that our God knows our great need. He is the Creator of our humanity. He knows your nature, your weaknesses, and your strengths. He cares about your secret longings and your dreams. He said to us, I am the God of all comfort.

> **Brave means that you turn to God for comfort. Brave does not mean enduring heartache and trouble all alone.**

I AM *Jehovah,* the eternal, ever-loving God.

I AM *Jehovah-Rophi,* the Lord, the physician.

I AM *Jehovah-Shalom,* the Lord, our peace.

I AM *El Olam,* the God of eternity.

Would you turn with me to 2 Corinthians 1:3-11?

What three names did Paul give to God?

1.

2.

3.

Just to add perspective, go back and write the words I AM in front of each of God's names.

To be honest with you, this passage wasn't my first choice for the week. I wanted to turn to a different place in the Bible to hear from God about my trembling. Maybe a chapter in Psalms where the writer asked God to remove an affliction. Maybe a miraculous healing passage or some place where angels appeared and said to the trembling, "Fear not." But God has led me here. This is a big passage with huge truth to absorb. It's a little like a "horse pill," as my mama used to call it. Good for you but kind of hard to swallow.

First, let's look at the main thing—who our God is. Paul wrote: "Praise be to the God and Father of our Lord Jesus Christ, the Father of compassion and the God of all comfort" (2 Cor. 1:3).

This week I want you to focus on these aspects of God's character: He is the Father of Jesus, your Savior; He is the God of compassion; and He is the God of all comfort. No matter your trouble. No matter your disease. No matter your hardship or problem or disappointment. No matter what makes you tremble inside. Only God can give a divine and powerful comfort that comes to us from the depths of His character.

People I love can give me **a portion** of comfort, but my deep, abiding {comfort **always comes from God.**}

If the people we love can only give a part of the comfort we long for but God can give all, maybe we should change our expectations toward others.

Have you expected that someone or something could comfort you fully? How did you feel when they didn't come through?

If other people cannot give what only God can give to us, could it be that many times we have looked to the wrong source for our peace and healing? From what wrong places or people have you sought comfort?

"The God of all comfort" (2 Cor. 1:3) means that God is able to bring ease and freedom from the pain, even in our sufferings. **How have you experienced a deeper comfort that could only come God?**

Look at this part of the passage in verses

3 & 4:

"Praise be to ...
the God of all comfort,
who comforts us in
all our troubles."

2 CORINTHIANS 1:3-4

Name three ways you can give a hurting person to stay connected to God.

1.
2.
3.

Even though our focus is on the God described in
2 Corinthians, know that all through Scripture
God is known as the God of comfort.
Take a look at these passages:

"Shout for joy, O heavens;
rejoice, O earth;
burst into song, O mountains!
For the LORD comforts his people
and will have compassion on his afflicted ones."

ISAIAH 49:13

"I, even I, am he who comforts you."

ISAIAH 51:12

"As a mother comforts her child,
so will I comfort you."

ISAIAH 66:13

Now fill in these blanks:

God gives ▨▨▨▨
the comfort we need in
▨▨▨▨▨▨ the troubles
we face.

What does it mean to you that God promises to comfort us "in all our troubles"?

"All comfort" means receiving **completely** what you need.

But to receive all that we need from God means that we must remain consistently connected to the One who gives all that we need. In our troubles, many times we are so consumed with finding an answer or healing a hurt that we forget to turn to God.

"Even though I walk
through the valley of the shadow of death,
I will fear no evil,
for you are with me;
your rod and your staff,
they comfort me."

PSALM 23:4

God of all comfort!

The day I drove home from my gynecologist with my knees shaking and my hands trembling, the first thing I did was call my husband. My call went to his voice mail. No answer. I decided I was going to drive to my house and get on my face to begin praying, but you know what happened? As I was making my plan for praying, even before I had earnestly begun to pray, God came to me. I kind of wanted to cry over my bad news, but no tears came because even though the human in me had been trembling, the soul of me realized that God was present. He was powerfully present.

How did I know? Because the deepest peace took hold of my trembling insides, and everything inside of me—heart, soul, and physical body—was at ease. Completely still. The trembling just stopped.

It was as if God breathed a peace over me even before I'd rustled up a good, long prayer. He gave me in a moment even more than I could have hoped for. It was, and is, exactly the kind of peace Paul wrote about to the Philippians: "And the peace of God, which transcends all understanding, will guard your hearts and your minds in Christ Jesus" (Phil. 4:7).

So, my sister, is your heart heavy today?

Is trouble brewing around you? Do you need a comfort only God can give? I'd love to pray for you.

God of all comfort, would You flood my sister's heart with the comfort that only You can give? Bring a peace that transcends her circumstances. Be powerful with Your presence and compassion. And Father, let Your Spirit calm every place inside of us that wants to tremble with fear.

Remind us to remember we belong to You. We are daughters of the God of all comfort. With gratefulness we seek You and praise You.

Amen.

DAY 3

THE PURPOSE OF RECEIVING COMFORT

Yesterday at the gym I talked to a woman who is 20 years younger than me. She is about seven months pregnant with her first child and a self-proclaimed perfectionist. She's my kind of woman. I have been her. We talked about paint in the baby's nursery. She found a picture she liked, and her dad and husband are doing the painting. So far, nothing looks like the picture. My overachieving, perfect Mama is devastated. She said she just stands in the nursery and wants to bawl. It's not turning out like she hoped. My heart ached for her. I remember feeling the same thing so many times. Still do sometimes.

My first right decision was not to give her the bad news. I didn't tell her that the paint is just the beginning and that life's disappointments keep coming long after the nursery becomes a cool teen bedroom. I didn't tell her that people are just people and they want to paint from your picture but most of the time it won't look exactly the same.

I told her I understood completely. Because I do. I told her I'd wanted perfection too. Because I did. One of life's most difficult lessons is living with finger paints when you were hoping for a Rembrandt. Surrender takes time, at least it sure did for me. A baby on the way is probably coming to teach my sweet-as-pie-control-freak-friend more about surrender than she ever planned on knowing.

After my last round of pitiful crunches, I looked at my friend and told her, "As hard as it is, you might have to let this one go even if it stings. In this world, people

Let's go back to
2 Corinthians 1 again today.

Read verses 3-10. What was Paul's focus? Was it on himself or on his hardships?

How does Paul's focus give perspective for your own present-day troubles or fears? Where is your focus today?

Reread verses 4-5. Note one of the amazing insights Paul gave us about our suffering:

> "[God] comforts us in all our affliction, so that we may be able to comfort those who are in any kind of affliction, through the comfort we ourselves receive from God.
> For as the sufferings of Christ overflow to us, so through Christ our comfort also overflows."
>
> 2 CORINTHIANS 1:4-5, HCSB

Paul said God uses our inward suffering to turn us outward toward others. How has your suffering done that for you?

matter more than paint. You don't want to wound the very ones you love. Believe me, the more days go by, the less you'll notice a few imperfections on the wall. Very soon, this baby girl is all you'll be able to see."

I know she heard me because I saw it in her eyes. She knew she wasn't alone and that she wasn't crazy for wanting the prettiest nursery a baby ever slept in. I tried to give her the comfort God has been so gracious to give me.

I left the gym grateful I could pass my notes back—that I could give something based on the very real lessons I've spent years learning with God. I hope I gave some comfort from the comfort God has given to me.

Amazing, when you stop to think about it. As much as pain makes us want to retreat and hide, Paul said we're supposed to receive the mercy of God's comfort and then turn toward a hurting world with all that has been given to us—a selflessness right in the middle of great suffering. It's just like God to say,

"Use your suffering to help someone else. Take the truth of My character to those who are hurting." Then He gives us the grace to make it happen.

Paul said that he prayed that his comfort to others would give them a "patient endurance" (2 Cor. 1: 6) in their trials.

How would you describe a "patient endurance"?

In the same way, I don't think God is asking us to hide our real emotions or fears. We just can't help how our humanity responds to heartache and suffering. The physical body gasps for air when we can't breathe just as the spiritual body gasps for grace when we are in need. Paul showed us how to be honest with our struggles and how to run to the God of all comfort with our fears.

Have you ever been under great pressure, far beyond your ability to endure? How so?

Take a look at verses 8-9:

"We were under great pressure, far beyond our ability to endure, so that we despaired even of life. Indeed, in our hearts we felt the sentence of death."

It is very brave to give the comfort you have been given.

Have you ever despaired for your very life? If so, please tell me a bit about it.

I love that Paul didn't sugar-coat anything. He was honest with his real troubles, feelings, and fears. He was vulnerable and plain-spoken, not trying to make himself sound spiritual and unattainable. He thought they were going to die.

Receiving comfort from God when you have been so afraid is exactly the kind of comfort that will minister to others. Think of a recent time when you gave someone else **the comfort God has given to you.**

Now look at Paul's understanding of his despair in verse 9: **"But this happened that we might not rely on ourselves but on God."**

Oh my goodness, if we could only weave this lesson into the fabric of our lives. The first thing I do when I encounter a trial is rely on myself. I look on the Internet to research solutions and procedures. I call people. Mentally I try to think through a logical approach.

What about you? What is your first response when trouble comes?

The Lord is so very compassionately teaching us to rely on Him and not on ourselves. I have been the slowest learner sometimes. I want to be the strong woman of God who instantly relies on Him, but I find myself the fretful woman of fear who jumps in with both feet to straighten everything out.

If I know anything, I know that God is the only hope I have. Bit by bit I am learning to remember that before I rush out to fix things myself. Receiving His comfort in my troubles and turning to give to someone else what God has given me beats relying on my own power every time.

As you've been studying this passage, has God brought to mind anyone you could comfort? A word or note might help them live with a "patient endurance." A call or an e-mail could encourage them to persevere. Maybe today is a day you are to receive the comfort of God, and maybe today is a day you give it away.

Listen as the Lord tells you what to do.

I've got to tell you, learning to rely on God is much more peaceful. Being held in God's strong arms of comfort is the sweetest place I know.

WHEN GOD IS SILENT

Some days God rushes in with the power of His presence. You can feel Him in the room. You know He's speaking to your heart, and nothing is more beautiful than your relationship with our high and holy God. You can bring Him your troubles and receive His comfort, and everything about the goodness of God fits inside your understanding.

Other times you find yourself trembling inside, longing for peace, a word from God, or the assurance of His presence, and God seems uncaringly silent. Maybe heaven seems far away. Maybe you feel God isn't speaking to you. Maybe you even think He's turned His back on you.

We've all been there at one time or another. Many days I've wanted God to paint a message across the wall, send me an e-mail, or speak out loud with a voice like thunder. Anything to tell me what to do, where to go, whom to trust. On some of those days I searched with all my heart and received nothing. God was quiet. No answers came.

We're not alone wondering where God is sometimes. Take time to read Psalm 22 from your Bible and keep it open to the psalm as we study today. Feeling abandoned by God, David, the man after God's own heart, penned the song questioning where God was and why.

I'm so grateful for the honesty in Scripture. David obviously knew what it felt like to wonder why. Have you ever felt like David—forsaken and far away from God?

David remembered others God didn't disappoint (v. 5). Then David poured out his troubles. He reported feeling scorned, despised, and mocked (vv. 6-7).

We've all been there. Look around. All you can see are people with answered prayers. Look at yourself. All you can see is your trouble and despair. Has life ever felt like that for you too?

PSALM 22

In the middle of this psalm, feeling abandoned by God, David chose to exercise his faith. Pay attention here because someday, somewhere, God will seem far away and we too will be required to exercise our faith.

In this passage David did six things we need to remember. He reminded himself who God is, how faithful He is, and who David was. Then he encouraged himself to look at his options, to hold on patiently, and to anticipate God's renewed presence. Let's look at each of those steps.

Don't forget!

1
Remind yourself who God is.

In verse 3 David remembered that God is _____.

In verse 9 he remembered God is his Creator and gave him _____.

In verse 19 he called God _____ _____.

2
Review God's faithfulness.

In verses 4-5 David reviewed God's faithfulness to the generations before him. If you took a minute to review God's faithfulness, what would you say? How has God been faithful to you?

The brave woman believes God is working, even when He is silent.

3

Recall who you are.

In verse 6 David recalled what others had said about him. He said that according to others he was a _____.

But in verses 9-10 he remembered who he was because of God. He recalled that God had had His eye on David before he was born.

Do you remember who God says you are today? Or do you focus on what you believe others think of you? I know which one is easier, but don't forget: Exercising your faith is a choice. You have to choose to recall who you are because of God or all you will think about is what others believe.

4

Evaluate other options.

David looked around to see what others were doing. He thought life seemed easier for everyone else (see Ps. 73).

Maybe you look around and somehow life seems easier for everyone else too.

Maybe you've tried everything else and found only dead-end streets apart from God. David came to the conclusion that no help would be coming from people (Ps. 22:11). God was his only help.

As you look at the other options in your own life, maybe you have realized that God is your only help. Even when God is silent and you can't hear Him speak, He is still your only answer.

5

Wait. Hold on.

By verse 19 David was waiting on God. He was holding on until God came to help him. "O my Strength, come quickly to help me."

Sometimes our faith must choose to hold on. We have to remember who God is, who He has been, and whose we are. Then we must hold on. Maybe today exercising your faith means you make the choice to hold on too.

6

Anticipate God's renewed presence.

At the end of Psalm 22 nothing about David's circumstances had changed. He was still surrounded by trouble, but David had changed. His faith had made a way for hope. In verses 27-31 he was anticipating the future. He was anticipating God's renewed presence and God's future goodness to him. He said in verse 31, "They will proclaim his righteousness to a people yet unborn—for he has done it."

While God was still silent, David exercised his faith and decided that one day people yet unborn would know that God came through. Wow. David's faith is such an incredible model for us.

When God is silent, do you anticipate His renewed presence, or do you give up and walk away?

Why do you think you react this way?

While on the cross what passage did Jesus quote regarding God's silence? (See Matt. 27:46; Mark 15:34.)

What did Jesus do even when He felt abandoned by God?

The future for every believer is greater things from God. When we anticipate the future with God, we can always count on the blessings of His character. We can be certain of that not merely because of David's example but because of Jesus. He also faced every temptation and suffering that we will encounter.

Where was Jesus when He felt abandoned by God?

Did you connect the dots?

From the cross Jesus quoted the words of David.

A couple of things I hope you never forget, even in the darkest, most quiet times are:

If God were going to abandon you, He never would have sent His Son.

If God were going to abandon you, Jesus never would have gone to the cross.

God may be silent for you today, but I pray for you, my friend, hold on.

DAY 5

BECOMING BRAVE

When faced with a fear that makes us cower, we have two options. We can continue in fear with increased trembling and decisions made from our insecurity. Or we can believe God, who He has been, who we know Him to be, and allow the promised comfort of His character to make us brave.

I love these beautiful words from Hannah Whitall Smith and hope they'll touch your heart too:

"Divine comfort does not come to us in any mysterious or arbitrary way. It comes as the result of a divine method. The indwelling Comforter brings to our remembrance comforting things concerning our Lord. If we believe them, we are comforted by them."[2]

In choosing to believe the truths concerning God, we remember His faithful character and put our hope in His faithfulness. We remember His sovereignty and surrender our troubles back to His control. Maybe most comforting to me has always been to remember God's sovereignty on this earth.

I'll never forget the first time I truly understood God's sovereignty. I'm sad to say I didn't really grasp it until I was in seminary. As the professors began to unfold this beautiful attribute of God in their teaching, I vividly remember the comfort that settled on my heart. God is in control. Oh, thank goodness. Hallelujah. God is sovereign.

Have you forgotten that God is in control? Does it give you comfort to remember that God is over all things, that nothing comes to you or to me apart from His watchful eye?

THE THEOLOGY OF GOD'S SOVEREIGNTY

We could take a lifetime with this truth and should. More and more I find that every passage of Scripture points to this one thing: **God has supreme, independent authority.** I think you'll find great comfort in these Scriptures. I also think the woman who believes in the sovereignty of God finds a quick comfort in her troubles. It's divine inner comfort and strength that take an ordinary woman and begin to make her brave.

> "The LORD has established His throne in the heavens, and His sovereignty rules over all."
>
> PSALM 103:19, NASB

The Bible teaches us that God is the Supreme Ruler and Authority over all that occurs in His kingdom and all creation. This big theological truth is like a doctrine of comfort to me. Sinful men or a fallen world do not determine my life's destiny. My life is under the authority of a loving, eternal God who does not flinch, doubt, or guess. Our God is completely in control, and that truth gives me such a deep peace. I am held. I am loved. I am protected.

For God to be sovereign means that He has unlimited command of all things. Look at these passages and circle the word "everything" wherever you read it.

"Our citizenship is in heaven. And we eagerly await a Savior from there, the Lord Jesus Christ, who, by the power that enables him to bring everything under his control, will transform our lowly bodies so that they will be like his glorious body" (Phil. 3:20-21).

"The Son radiates God's own glory and expresses the very character of God, and he sustains everything by the mighty power of his command" (Heb. 1:3, NLT).

To be sovereign means that God is in authority over_____.

He works out everything.
He brings everything
under His lordship.
He sustains everything.

God's sovereignty means that whatever trouble or fear you are facing, whatever makes you tremble inside, God is able to …

work it out

bring it under His control

sustain you through it

Take a look at how Paul said we can respond to the sovereignty of God:

> "Yet he did not waver through unbelief regarding the promise of God, but was strengthened in his faith and gave glory to God, being fully persuaded that God had power to do what he had promised."
>
> ROMANS 4:20-21

According to Romans 4:20-21, those who put faith in God's control do the following:

- We do not waver through unbelief.
- We are strengthened in our faith.
- We give glory to God.
- We are fully persuaded that God has power to fulfill His promises.

When you read those four attitudes of a woman who is resting in the sovereignty of God, how do you fare today?

Goodness, I didn't realize I'm not trusting.

I'm getting there.

I've put the weight of my troubles on His promises.

God is too wise to make a mistake. God is too good to be unkind.

—Babbie Mason

As we've walked through this week together, I hope you've examined the places where you feel afraid. I hope you've been honest about everything that makes you tremble inside. I pray that you've encountered the God of all comfort in a way that strengthens your faith.

Sometimes the presence of God rushes in and immediately gives you a peace that transcends all understanding. Sometimes God is present but silent, requiring us to exercise our faith. But in all things, God is sovereign, in authority, the Ruler of everything that concerns us.

Will you receive the comfort God promises, no matter how He chooses to give it to you? Sometimes when I have been overwhelmed and discouraged, I began praying: *God, I need something. I don't even know what I need, but I need to know that You're here. That You have a plan. That You are moving in the unseen.*

Then I began to watch for God. Maybe days will go by, but always, always, God has answered my prayer. I know He has answered when my spirit has lifted and hope has been restored. Sometimes He has used a phone call. Many times He has answered when I read a passage of Scripture. God has been very creative with His comfort to me through the years. But I tell you, God keeps His promises, and He always stays true to His character.

He is the God of all comfort. Would you ask Him to comfort you today?

i am trembling inside

2 Corinthians 1:3

I AM the God of all _____.

He is the _____ of all comfort. He is the _____ where comfort is manufactured.

Comfort to our soul happens in the _____ of God.

2 Corinthians 1:4-5

The purpose of receiving comfort is so that we may _____ others.

2 Corinthians 1:6

We comfort others to give them a _____ _____ in their trials.

2 Corinthians 1:8-9

We go through difficult times so that we might _____ to rely on God and not on ourselves.

Note: Angela quotes from Hannah W. Smith, *The God of All Comfort* , [cited 20 October 2010]. Available from the Internet: *http://www.raptureready.com/resource/smith/vv3.htm*

Video sessions are available for download at *www.lifeway.com/women*

WEEK 5

· · · · · · · · · · · · · · · · · ·

i am invisible

Let me describe an experience I think we've all had. You attend a party or a reception where a variety of people will be. You strike up a conversation with a person who seems interesting enough, but the whole time you are interacting, the other person keeps glancing over your head, occasionally looking around you, anywhere but directly at you. Then you realize, *Oh, she's looking for someone else. Someone she would enjoy talking to more.*

I can't begin to count how many times that has happened to me, especially at professional gatherings. Then the moment comes when the someone more important is spotted. The conversation ends abruptly with a quick "Let's catch up another time," and I'm left standing there. Years ago I took those abrupt endings personally—like they were a declaration of my value or lack of it. I would turn toward the rest of the room feeling incredibly unspecial and fairly invisible.

Thank goodness for the truth of God and its power to transform our responses. I am learning that other people don't necessarily speak for God. Because I am not invisible to Him, these days I can be in a crowded room of strangers and remember I am seen by the only One who really matters.

Being ignored and feeling unnoticed at a reception is one thing, but to live most days not believing you are worthy to be known is a special kind of torture. Sometimes that's how we allow this world to make us feel.

Maybe I'm not the only one and you too have felt the sting of invisibility. Let's do some Bible study together on this tough but honest question: "Lord, do You know I feel invisible?"

UNSEEN

Invisible isn't a new role for most women. We've all experienced it. When I have two or three 12-year-old girls in my car, it's amazing how quickly I become invisible to them. Somehow the car is going where they would like to go, but they have no idea that I am there steering the vehicle. Not only can they not see me but they can't even hear me. Then there are the nights of boys and food. Teenage boys run inside, they eat in a happy fury, and they are gone again, unaware that the whole time I was standing there pouring their drinks and handing them napkins. Invisible. Yep, moms know all about invisible.

Maybe you have walked into a new class at school and felt invisible. Maybe you sit in a cubicle at your job, certain that no one can see the amazing woman just on the other side of your partitioned walls. Maybe you lie in a bed every night beside the husband who barely notices. Maybe you rock your baby alone in the night, and your love and hard work feel invisible. No one sees. No one applauds. No one gives you a hug or an *Atta girl!*

Almost everyone I know has felt the pang of invisibility. Some of us live with that heartache every day. Maybe you've heard your heart shout to God, "Do You know I am invisible down here?"

Brave women keep showing up every day, even when no one sees and no one says thank you.

When have you experienced feeling invisible?

Maybe people see you and walk around you at the grocery store, but the soul can fill with loneliness and sometimes we wonder:

Do you know who I am?
Does anyone see the real me inside?
Do you think that I'm special?
Am I worth the time it would take to get to know me?
Does someone care what makes me laugh? what dreams I dream?

As you think of the women you know and the life you have lived, what other honest questions do women ask when they feel invisible?

Last night I had the great privilege of speaking to 600 Christian women speakers and writers. It was a thrill to look around the room, knowing we're on the same team, each called with individual gifts to be used for God's purposes. I felt like I had the opportunity to pass my notes to them. Maybe if they could avoid something I had to learn the hard way, the message God has given them could be heard sooner and with greater passion.

One of the things I cautioned them about is unfair comparison. I felt like they could be tempted to look across the banquet table and begin to quietly compare their gifts to the woman across the table. And because we are all wired about the same, in the game of unfair comparison we all come up short.

I have many times unfairly compared myself to someone else. Her gifts. Her lifestyle. Her skinny jeans. Every time I do it, I always lose in my mind.

How about you?
Do you secretly play the comparison game too? How do you play your version?

When we begin to compare ourselves to another woman in the room, we can quickly decide that we are invisible and she is not. We are less. She is more. We are insecure. She is confident. We are wanna be's. She has arrived. From that stinky, invisible place, the soul can do one of three things. Maybe one of the most brave and

sad things I can tell you is that I have done them all. But I really believe I'm growing up now. These first two are embarrassing, but here goes.

1. STRIVING

When I have felt invisible, one of the things I have unconsciously done is what I call striving. Striving is an ugly thing, especially on a godly woman. Ever met a woman who was trying too hard? Striving. Talking too much? Striving. Giving her manuscript to anyone who would stand still or who couldn't get away? Striving. I have been a striving woman. Mostly my striving came from fear—the fear of being invisible.

For me, striving means looking around and unfairly comparing myself to someone else or to many. When I am living for my audience of One, then I remember that I am known and seen by God. When I am unfocused, looking around and comparing, I quickly feel invisible to others and to God.

Can you add a few more characteristics of a striving woman?

How have you struggled with striving? trying to make things happen? helping God out? forcing what you long for into being?

When we feel unnoticed, we can begin to believe God doesn't see us either. Have you ever felt invisible to God?

2. SULKING

The first few years I attended Bookseller Conventions I walked around with my little books feeling completely unseen and totally insignificant. I would look up at the giant posters of my Bible-teaching heroes and wonder what in the world I was doing there. I was the person someone would politely talk to until a more important person walked in. I'm sure you've known the same feeling. After those weekends I would get on a plane with my sulking heart and decide to quit. Who needed another book anyway? And everyone else was really godly and great. What was I thinking?

So many times, when I have felt invisible, I have chosen the path of sulking. Giving up. Do you know what sulking does for an invisible woman? It makes her feel even more invisible.

Have you ever chosen the path of sulking? If so, tell me about it.

Has sulking ever helped anything feel better for you?

I told you these first two paths have been embarrassing. It's so amazing what feeling invisible will convince you to do. Thankfully, God is teaching me a much better way to deal with the temptation of comparison.

3. SEEKING

My life verse is Matthew 6:33: "Seek first his kingdom and his righteousness, and all these things will be given to you as well."

I have applied this verse to many decisions since my college days, and it has always guided me and given me strength. Then one day God spoke this verse over my invisible heart. It's like He said to me, "You do not have to choose striving or sulking when you feel invisible. You can seek Me instead."

That's what we're going to do this week. Seek Him. We will practice seeking His kingdom and His righteousness, and all these things will be given to us. What things? The things our hearts long for—like being seen when we feel invisible.

Let's take a minute and tell the Lord our struggles:

Oh God, I have felt invisible when:

And, I have felt invisible to these people:

Sometimes, when I felt that way, I have chosen:

But this week, Lord, I choose to seek You.

Will You find me and tell me that You see me?

With a heart full of expectation. I love You.

Amen and amen.

RUNNING AWAY

The Old Testament tells a story about a downcast woman named Hagar. Today we're going to pick up her story in Genesis 16 with the narrative of Abram and Sarai. Before we learn more about Hagar, maybe it would help to have a little background information.

God promised Abram he would have a son and that his descendants would outnumber the stars in the heavens. The Bible says that Abram believed God. But the years went by and no son ever came. So Abram's wife, Sarai, decided to take matters into her own hands and offered him Hagar, her Egyptian maidservant. In that ancient culture a barren wife could give a slave to her husband, but this act wasn't what God intended. Sarai was trying to get ahead of the Lord. Like so many of us, she misinterpreted God's delay as a denial and took matters into her own hands.

I already see myself in this story.

I have been disappointed with God's timing.
I have tried to get ahead of God.
I have misinterpreted God many times.
For the record, I have never given my servant to my husband.

GOODNESS.

How about you?
Do you see yourself in this story too?

The story continues, and Hagar conceived a child with Abram, only to find Sarai horribly jealous during her pregnancy. The Scripture says: "Then Sarai mistreated Hagar; so she fled from her" (Gen. 16:6).

Hagar's name means *flight,* so in the face of abuse and humiliation, she did exactly as her name implied. Hagar ran away, out into the wilderness.

This world can make you want to run away, but the brave woman stays, living every day with integrity.

Hagar was in despair, hopeless, weary, alone, a woman in a male-dominated culture, pregnant, rejected, cast out after being used, surely feeling no one cared for her. No one understood.

Verse 7 says: "The angel of the LORD found Hagar near a spring in the desert; it was the spring that is beside the road to Shur."

I'm not sure where the road to Shur would have taken Hagar, but I am absolutely sure that she believed anywhere was better than the awful circumstances she was enduring. As Hagar sat that day beside a spring in the desert, she felt incredibly alone. Unseen. Invisible to the people who knew her, and surely believing that she was invisible to God.

I don't know if your circumstances ever made you want to run into a desert, but I know mine have. I remember times in my divorce and single-mom life when anywhere else seemed better than where I was, even if it was under a tree in a desert.

Have you ever felt like anywhere else would be better than where you are now? If so, tell me about it.

Where are you going when you think about leaving it all and hiding from your problems? I usually choose Africa or Montana. Of course, some island far away always sounds peaceful too.

Maybe you have endured a judgment that made you want to evaporate. Just ask any Christian woman who has suffered through a divorce. She'll tell you what judgment feels like. Or ask the Christian woman who admits to having had an abortion, an affair, or an addiction. She knows that the heat of the desert seems mild compared to the heat of scandal, disgrace, and gossip.

Maybe you've never packed a bag but you've run away in your heart. You have disconnected from your husband, your children, and your church. Maybe you have decided to endure those who have hurt you, but for all intents and purposes, you have run away, you and your hardened heart, and put up a tent in the desert that is called your life.

Maybe you have a girlfriend who has emotionally run into a desert. Or maybe the desert dweller is you. Just like Hagar, it takes a lot of hurt to make a desert become the better option. So much hurt upon hurt can begin to convince you that no one cares, not even God. The hurt and disappointment lie to you and call you invisible. Today God tells you the truth.

Can you understand how very real hurt will tell you lies until the mind decides to believe them? What lies have you heard and believed from your pain?

The glory of God stepped into the desert that day with Hagar. Right to Hagar's side, God sent an "angel of the LORD." Many theologians believe this was a preincarnate appearance of the very presence of God's Son, Jesus. God saw Hagar hiding in the desert that day. God sees you and me. We are not invisible to Him.

Today I am sitting in my study in my one comfy chair. The dogs are bugging the life out of me, growling at the window and begging me to move over. I have an afghan over my feet because I'm cold. My computer is propped on my knees, and my Bible is open to Genesis 16 beside me. I am alone, but not really. My kids keep texting me about when to pick up who and where. I am not in a desert today, but as I've looked around my room, I've said to the Lord, *I want Your glory here.* I am not in Shur today, but I've been there. Even on this day of relative peace, I long to be seen by God. I want to know His glory and walk under His gaze.

Maybe you long to be seen by God too. The most beautiful truth I could tell you is that God has never looked away. He neither blinks, dozes, nor naps. He is the God who sees. He sees you, and He sees me.

PLEASE PUT YOUR NAME IN EVERY BLANK SPACE BELOW:

"[_____,] He who watches over you will not slumber; indeed, he who watches over Israel will neither slumber nor sleep. [_____,] the LORD watches over you—the LORD is your shade at your right hand; the sun will not harm you by day, nor the moon by night. [_____,] the LORD will keep you from all harm—he will watch over your life; the LORD will watch over your coming and going both now and forevermore" (Ps. 121:3-8).

Amen.

THE GOD WHO SEES

Take a minute to close your eyes and remember that wherever you are, however your day has been, no matter your circumstances, God sees you.

This morning I am upstairs with my door closed and listening to the voices in my house. The kids are waking up and talking to each other. The dogs are barking. Someone's radio is playing down the hall. Four cable repairmen are outside talking. Not one of them realizes I am here. Propped against the foot of my bed, begging God for His anointing. I am unseen. Except that I know God is here. He sees me. He is guiding me. He loves me.

I am praying for you this morning—that you know God's nearness. He sees you. Even more importantly, His love for you is never-ending.

Yesterday we closed our books with Hagar in a desert, alone and afraid. But thankfully, she was not abandoned. The angel of the Lord had arrived. The very presence of God had come to a despised woman with a message.

I hope that gives you hope today. God comes to rescue even those our society has shunned—the invisible. According to Genesis 16:9-10, the angel of the Lord came to Hagar with an instruction and a promise.

What instruction did God give Hagar (v. 9)?

What was God's promise to Hagar (v. 10)?

The angel of the Lord gave Hagar a deep comfort by telling her that He saw her plight: "You are now with child and you will have a son. You shall name him Ishmael, for the LORD has heard of your misery" (v. 11).

Even though Hagar must surely have felt invisible to everyone else, she encountered God in the most barren of places. God saw her loneliness, and He heard her cries.

God is a personal God. He is your personal God. Maybe you need to know that He is concerned with abused women and unborn babies. The psalmist reminded us that this is the very character of God, to see our pain and bring encouragement and strength in our suffering: "You hear O LORD, the desire of the afflicted; you encourage them, and you listen to their cry" (Ps. 10:17).

Do you need some encouragement today? This morning I received a two-line e-mail with such sweet encouragement. It really stirred my soul and reminded me that every one of us could use a little encouragement. I wish I could be there with you to give you a hug or pour you a cup of coffee. But even better, I can point you to the One who is near. I can give you some of the verses that encourage me. Just pretend like I'm sitting there reading these to you:

"My God will meet all your needs according to his glorious riches in Christ Jesus."
PHILIPPIANS 4:19

"You will keep in perfect peace him whose mind is steadfast, because he trusts in you."
ISAIAH 26:3

> When an everyday woman remembers she's seen by God, He makes the very soul of that woman brave.

> *"For God did not give us a spirit of timidity (of cowardice, of craven and cringing and fawning fear), but [He has given us a spirit] of power and of love and of calm and well-balanced mind and discipline and self-control."*
> 2 TIMOTHY 1:7, AMPLIFIED

> *"Cast your burden on the Lord [releasing the weight of it] and He will sustain you; He will never allow the [consistently] righteous to be moved (made to slip, fall, or fail)."*
> PSALM 55:22, AMPLIFIED

It's just come to me as I'm typing these verses. Do you know someone who needs encouragement? You don't even have to have the right words to say. Maybe you can type one of the above verses into an e-mail and push send. A little thing for your friend who needs to know God sees her too.

I believe God sees our heartache and our pain, and He desires to intervene in our lives with mercy, instruction, and promise. I also believe that many times in our own private deserts the tears we cry when we cannot speak reach the heart of our Father as well as the prayers we are able to form with our minds. I don't know if Hagar had been in the desert praying, but I can imagine she had been there crying in her misery. After the angel of the Lord had compassionately spoken to Hagar, the Bible says, "She gave this name to the LORD who spoke to her: 'You are the God who

sees me,' for she said, 'I have now seen the One who sees me'" (Gen. 16:13).

I can just imagine Hagar crying out with joy to God, "You really, really see me. You have seen my sadness, my confusion, and my pain. Oh God, thank You, thank You! Surely, You are the God who sees."

I once read about a medical study of the brain. The article said that in the front part of the brain lies a joy center that lights up when we experience joy. Do you know when each of the study participants felt joy? When they walked into a room where someone was happy to see them. Being seen and loved gives us such great joy. It lights up the brain.

> **Think about how it makes you feel when someone is happy to see you. What adjectives describe what goes on in your brain?**

Can you imagine how Hagar's joy center must have lit up when the angel of the Lord came to her? I pray it gives you a deep joy to know you too are seen and loved by the Most High God.

From Hagar's great joy over God's presence and His words, she named Him *El Roi,* the God who sees. When Hagar named God in this passage, she began the Old Testament custom of giving a new name to God when He appeared to His people. Hagar also marked the spot where she encountered God with a well she named "The God who sees me."

I AM

I AM *El Roi,*
the God who sees.

I AM *Jehovah Rohi,*
the Lord my shepherd.

Based on what God is doing in your life, what name would you give to Him?

As we wrap up, I think it's important to highlight this Old Testament custom. Hagar made a big deal out of her encounter with the angel of the Lord. She gave God a new name. Are you making a big deal out of the presence of God? We live on the other side of the Old Testament where God's presence never leaves us. We can live every day with the fullness and indwelling of the Holy Spirit. We have the privilege of an intimate relationship with our Lord.

I'm not going to give you any ideas on this one because I think you'll be more creative without my prompts.

What are some ways that we can build modern-day monuments to the glory of God?

You may be standing in the light of God's glory, and you know that He sees you. You are watching Him move in your life. You can trace His hand across your journey. If that's you, how about a little shout, "Hallelujah"?

Some of you are alone in the desert today.
I want you to know God is coming to your rescue!
Turn your heart toward the truth of Scripture.
God sees you even if you can't see Him. He knows
your great need. He has not abandoned you.
He is faithful to keep His promises to you too.
Even if you can't shout today, how about a whisper
based on faith, "Hallelujah"?

YOU ARE NOT INVISIBLE TO GOD

Last night my daughter Taylor drove a friend to the hospital. Her friend had purposely taken 10 times the amount of her prescription drug and then decided to call for help. Even in the hospital bed Taylor's friend cried and kept saying she wanted to die. The doctors attended this woman, and thankfully she is going to recover. But her mind and her heart need more time to mend. I am so very sad for her pain. The loneliness she must feel. The emptiness that left her without hope. You may have experienced the same kind of desperate darkness.

Many times I have heard women describe their battles with depression. They tell of a darkness so black that they feel like a light will never break through. The journey many times involves counseling, stays in the hospital, and necessary medication. I can only imagine that when the soul is that dark, it must feel like God cannot see.

Have you ever known the desperate darkness of depression or loved someone who struggles with it?

One more thing to tell you about Taylor's friend—she was baptized as a follower of Jesus Christ three days ago. Lord, surround Your daughter with Your presence today. She needs to see You.

From her most desperate circumstances, Hagar ran into a desert. While Hagar escaped from Abram and Sarai, Hagar did not escape *El Roi,* the God who sees. He knew right where she was, and He knew what she had been through. He came to Hagar, comforted her, gave her directions for survival, and spoke His promise of blessing to her.

Think of five words to describe your perspective of depression:

1.
2.
3.
4.
5.

> Trusting in the presence of God every day is a very brave thing to do.

If I could talk to Taylor's friend, I'd want her to know that God is still *El Roi*, the God who sees. He is there for her. He sees every tear. He hears every cry. He longs to heal her hurts. I pray she knows the real truth of this passage: "The LORD is close to the brokenhearted and saves those who are crushed in spirit" (Ps. 34:18).

Maybe you have known an abuse—sexual, mental, or physical—that has already driven you into a lonely desert. Maybe you suffer with depression and anxiety that keeps you prisoner in a desert. Maybe your own choices have caused you so much embarrassment that you have run into a desert to hide.

I want you to know that no matter how this world may have broken your heart, God is close, coming to save all who are crushed in spirit. The Bible makes a promise to everyone who turns toward God: "For you, LORD, have never forsaken those who seek you" (Ps. 9:10).

God never forsakes any who call out to Him. He sees your pain and does not turn away. God came to Hagar, and He will come to you.

That day in the desert, the angel of the Lord came to Hagar with instruction, a promise, and encouragement. From her great joy in meeting God, Hagar named God *El Roi*. But maybe the most important thing that Hagar did was to respond to God's instruction with obedience. She returned to Abram and Sarai as God had told her to do. She gave birth to Abram's son, Ishmael (whose name means "God hears"), and then lived in the promise of God's faithfulness.

That day God told Hagar to return to the place of her pain and wait for His promised faithfulness. Can you imagine what Hagar must have been thinking? Maybe she thought: *Could I get a different instruction from the angel of the Lord? That was not what I wanted to hear.* How many times have we heard from God about our own hurts and probably felt the same way? But even with the difficult task assigned to her, Hagar obeyed God. He kept His promise and blessed her.

I may have told women a million times that the whole Book of Proverbs can be summed up with these two equations:

Obedience to God = Blessing
Disobedience = Consequences

Hagar was obedient, and God blessed her.

I want us to camp out here for a little while with some instruction about obedience. I think I just heard someone say, "I wanted her to camp on the blessing."

First, maybe it would be great for you to write your own definition of obedience. What does obedience mean to you?

The *Tyndale Bible Dictionary* defines obedience this way: "The act or instance of submitting to the restraint or command of an authority; compliance with the demands or requests of someone over us."[1]

E. M. Bounds described obedience like this: "In principle, obedience to God is the same quality as obedience to earthly parents. It implies, in general effect, the giving up of one's own way, and following that of another; the surrendering of the will to the will of another; the submission of oneself to the authority and requirements of a parent."[2]

Do you think of obedience to God like a child being obedient toward a loving Father?

In just the same way, we are called to live in obedience as an act of honor toward the One who sees us, saves us, and loves us with an everlasting love. Obedience to God is our faith in action, the overflow of our love and gratefulness.

Remember that the most important thing Hagar did was to obey the God who sees. Take a few minutes to quietly search your heart.

Do you hesitate in your obedience? Do you have any obstacles that keep you from obeying? Do you suffer the consequences of disobedience?

CONSIDER WHERE YOU ARE WITH GOD:

quick and happy to obey God	slow and resentful	hit-or-miss obedience	flat-out refusal

No matter what you just answered, I want you to know you are not invisible to God. He is the God of your desert. He has instructions and promise. He will give encouragement on your journey. He longs to bless your obedience.

> *"Oh, that their hearts would be inclined to fear me and keep all my commands always, so that it might go well with them and their children forever!"*
> DEUTERONOMY 5:29

LET'S GIVE SOME THOUGHT TO THE JOURNEY WE'VE TAKEN THESE PAST FOUR DAYS.

A woman ran into a desert, lonely, abused, and feeling invisible.

The God of heaven came to find her.

He gave her instruction, a promise, and encouragement.

She named Him *El Roi*.

His love and faithfulness moved her to act in obedience.

LIVING IN HIS SIGHT

Hey, my friend, here is the great, great news of this week. God shouts to us, "Do you know I am the God who sees?" Even though this world and even the people we love can sometimes make us feel invisible, the amazing truth is that we are not unseen by God. He is where you are right now. He is powerfully present and delivering His instruction and promises for those who will listen.

Close your eyes and meditate on God's presence.
Read this passage and pray it back to God:

" 'Am I only a God nearby,' declares the LORD, 'and not a God far away? Can anyone hide in secret places so that I cannot see him?' declares the LORD. 'Do not I fill heaven and earth?' declares the LORD" (Jer. 23:23-24).

Praying back to God might begin something like this:
God, I know You are near ...

A WORD ABOUT JOURNALING

Journaling is a beautiful tool for insight and application. It's an amazing way to pray and remember God's goodness toward us. I have loved journaling in many seasons of my life but felt guilty when I did not journal. **Here is the one thing I read that gave me freedom: Jesus did not journal.** *Oh my, are you kidding? How did I miss that? How did I take a beautiful expression and make it a rule? Journaling is not a command. The Bible gives other commands that matter so much more. Things like "Love the LORD your God with all your heart" (Deut. 6:5). Journaling is a really great idea sometimes for some people.*

I don't know if you journal, but maybe you can use this space to jot some thoughts about your personal response to the Jeremiah passage above. How does your soul respond to this truth?

I'm praying some of you recovering rulekeepers just felt another chain snap!

Consider how Hagar returned to Abram and Sarai after she knew she was under the watchful care of God:

> She returned in obedience, even to difficult circumstances.

> She returned with her heart set on God, desiring to live for Him and know Him more.

> She returned with expectancy and hope for God's promises fulfilled.

> She returned grateful to be seen and loved by God.

We who are seen by God can live with our hearts wrapped around these same principles. God is glorified when we live every day aware and changed by His presence.

Name one negative connotation you associate with obedience.

1. BECAUSE GOD SEES, LET US LIVE IN OBEDIENCE.

We talked about obedience yesterday, but I want us to take a few more steps with this crucial directive. The woman who understands God's love for her wants to honor God's love with her obedience. I realize that just the word can conjure up all kinds of negative ideas and experiences for you.

Forced obedience to a dishonorable person.

Unreasonable obedience to a set of rules.

Excessive punishment for disobedience.

The call to obedience in Scripture is neither forced nor unreasonable. Our obedience is a by-product of love: God's love for us and our love for Him. Jesus said, "You are my friends if you do what I command" (John 15:14).

What we always have to keep in mind is that God's commandments, His instruction, and His direction for us come from the goodness of His character. God loves us with an everlasting love. He plans for our prosperity and promises not to harm us. He gives us a hope and a future and so much more. (See Jer. 29:11.)

> The brave woman responds to God's goodness with her obedience.

123

How does God's good heart toward you shape your attitude toward obedience to Him?

Do you want to be an amazing mom? A woman devoted to God will become one.

Do you need help for your marriage? A woman devoted to God will receive help.

Do you crave relationship and friendship? A woman devoted to God will be taught how to navigate healthy friendships.

Do you long to use your gifts for His glory? A woman devoted to God will be led.

Will a woman devoted to God lead a perfect life without mistakes or heartache? I can testify to this one: NO! But a woman devoted to God will be led, redirected, protected, guided, and blessed along the way. With my heart set on God, I am learning God's lessons for me on my imperfect journey. So thankful to be living in His sight along the way.

Where is God calling you to greater obedience? How will you respond to God based on His love?

2. BECAUSE GOD SEES, LET US LIVE WITH HEARTS SET ON GOD.

"Now devote your heart and soul to seeking the Lord your God" (1 Chron. 22:19).

I can't think of a better way to spend my life than devoted to seeking God. Here's what I know: Everything—and I mean everything—that you need comes from a devoted relationship to God.

3. BECAUSE GOD SEES, LET US LIVE WITH EXPECTANCY AND HOPE.

My seminary professor, Dr. Howard Hendricks, taught me many truths that shaped me as a woman, teacher, and follower of Christ. One of the sweetest things he taught me was to pray with expectancy. I love how that man prayed before and after our classes, always telling the Lord that we prayed and sought Him with expectancy. Truly it changes everything about the way you perceive God, to realign your prayers expecting Him to show up in His glory.

To live with **expectancy** means we learn to **engage our faith.**

Where is God asking you to engage your faith today?

Are you living with expectancy? Are you praying with expectancy and hope? How would it change everything for you to live each minute expecting God?

Let's pray an application of Ephesians 3:20 together with great faith and expectancy. **You can fill in the blank.**

God, I am struggling today with faith in this area: _____. Today I am engaging my faith over this concern. I am trusting that You are able to do immeasurably more than all I can ask or imagine according to Your power that is at work within me. I am giving You glory in advance as I learn to pray with expectancy and hope.

4. BECAUSE GOD SEES, LET US LIVE GRATEFULLY.

"Let them give thanks to the LORD for his unfailing love and his wonderful deeds for men, for he satisfies the thirsty and fills the hungry with good things" (Ps. 107:8-9).

Living gratefully reshapes the soul. A few weeks ago my friend Lysa TerKeurst gave a wonderful message at a conference where we were speaking. She talked about the dailyness of our lives and how we forget the goodness of God. She said she's reframing her life with gratefulness and instead of moaning, learning to rejoice with this kind of attitude:

Instead of saying, "I have to unload the dishwasher," grateful says, "I am able to unload the dishwasher."

Instead of, "I have to take my kids to soccer practice," grateful rejoices, "I am able to drive these people anywhere they need to go."

You see how this goes? What would some grateful "I am able" declarations look like from you today?

I AM ABLE TO:

This space is probably not enough. I'm praying this truth makes a home in your soul and for the rest of the day you hear your grateful heart declaring,

"Oh thank God, I am able."

Our God sees.

He directs.

He goes with us.

He promises.

Let us live like women who know God sees!

Session 6 Viewer Guide
GENESIS 16

Genesis 16:1-6

Hagar must have surely felt _____ to everyone, especially God.

Genesis 16:7-15

But God _____ Hagar (v. 7).

"The angel of the LORD" is a _____, which means God Himself is present.

God gives Hagar an _____:
 "Go back to your mistress and _____ to her" (v. 9).

God gives Hagar a _____:
 "Your _____ ... will be too numerous to count" (v. 10).

Hagar gives God the name _____, which means the God who _____ me (v. 13).

More importantly, Hagar gives God her _____.

WEEK 6

I AM BROKEN

Before I finished writing this study, I had the great privilege of teaching it at my home church in Greensboro, North Carolina. At the beginning of our sessions, I told the women I was praying about which topic to study for the last week. I gave them a few options and asked for feedback. Overwhelmingly they told me, "Do the week about broken."

I listened.

A few months ago Matthew West and I decided to write a devotional book together based on his recording titled "The Story of Your Life." Matthew had the brilliant idea to ask people to send him their stories. He told them to send anything. He put no restrictions on them. The story could be happy, sad, an accomplishment, a defeat, anything. Matthew told his fans he would read their stories and write songs based on many of them. What he didn't anticipate was receiving over 10,000 stories before he had to stop accepting new ones.

My family met Matthew on his tour bus one weekend to hang out, talk about the book, and to listen to some of his songs. As we talked, Matthew said that he had been blown away by the response of people all over the world who just wanted a chance to tell their stories. He was also stunned that the overwhelming majority of the stories were from women who had suffered sexual abuse. For all those women he wrote the song "Broken Girl." My tears fell while he played it. There are so many broken girls.

Brokenness comes to women through all kinds of abuse, but it comes to us in a million other ways too. A lot of you know my story, and you know that much of my brokenness came through separation and divorce. But my girlfriend's brokenness came with the birth of her autistic son. More women than I can count suffer their brokenness because of their husband's affair. Many more are broken by poor health, cancer, and the death of someone they love. A friend adopted a beautiful son, but his brokenness has made him a difficult child, almost more than his parents can bear. Their hearts and home are broken.

Our list of broken hearts, broken lives, and broken dreams could go on and on. The dictionary says that broken means:

- having been fractured or damaged and no longer in one piece or in working order
- rejected, defeated, or despairing
- sick or weakened
- a relationship ended by betrayal or faithlessness
- a family disrupted or divided
- a promise not kept

I am grateful to tell you that God does not flinch away from broken women; He moves closer. He does not shake His holy head in disgust. His compassion endures forever. He does not expect you to save yourself from your brokenness. He sent a Savior, Jesus, to redeem the world.

As I was reading through my dictionary for definitions of *broken*, my heart pounded a little harder when I read the antonym—*whole*. May this week be a week of healing and rejoicing for all of us. Our God says: I am your Redeemer.

I am praying that our Redeemer makes you whole. Let the redeemed of the Lord say so!

My Kung Pao Life

Don't miss our group time together through video this week. I wish I could be there in the flesh. I'm going to tell you the whole story about what's become one of our family's laugh lines. We got a plate of kung pao chicken that set us all afire. Through all our laughter, tears, and nose wiping, I said to the girls, "I think we got way more pao than kung." Now we can't eat that dish again without asking the waiter for a little less pao. The waiter never gets our joke, but we always think we are hilarious.

I think the whole idea of too much pao is a fairly typical experience for a lot of us. Most of us were just moseying along, ordering a medium spicy, very safe kind of life, then along came much more pao than anyone could swallow. *Way more pao than kung.* Or at least that's how it happened for me.

Maybe this isn't the life you ordered either. How has pao (more commonly known as brokenness) happened for you?

This morning I began my day with a mini-study of Psalm 34. I'd love for you to grab your Bible and a pen and jump in with me.

The psalmist, David, had many troubles and brokenness in his life, one of which was being detained by Achish, the king of the Philistines (1 Sam. 21:10-14). To gain his release, David pretended he was insane. Achish wanted nothing to do with another madman and released him.

Psalm 34 is David's reflection on God's goodness in our troubles and provides a perfect place for us to start. No matter what you are struggling with today or what kind of broken woman you are, I believe we should begin in praise like David did. Look at verses 1-3 and answer the following:

Whom did David want to hear this song of praise (v. 2)?

What did David want us, the afflicted, to do with him (v. 3)?

Can you glorify the name of God with me? Write a one-line psalm of praise to God:

David realized his own cleverness didn't gain his release from the Philistine king. Rather, it was God answering his prayers.

According to verse 4, what did David do?

And according to the same verse, what two things did God do?

1.

2.

I love verse 5. No matter where you are, where you have been, or what you have done, when you look to God, how does He see you?

1.

2.

I want to stop for a minute and jump up and down. Do you see the beauty of God's character? His deep, deep love for us? Even in our troubles and our broken places, when you turn toward God, you are radiant to Him. You never have to cover your face with shame. Oh bless the Lord. He is so good to us.

David went on to say in verse 6 that he was like everybody else facing trouble. "This poor man called, and the LORD heard him." David was at the bottom of the heap when he called on God. Maybe you feel like a poor woman today. Poor in spirit. Poor in ambition. Poor in love. But you can turn your poor spirit toward God and call on Him.

Remember the angel of the Lord who visited Hagar in our lesson last week? The angel was the very presence of God who came to guide and instruct her. In verse 7 David said the same "angel of the LORD encamps around those who fear him." That means God is with you too. The same deliverance that David experienced is available to you and me. God is not removed and far away; He is present, camping in a mobile home, and moving on this journey with the people whose hearts turn toward Him.

What does the angel of the Lord do (v. 7)?

The brave woman picks up all her broken pieces and places each in the strong hands of God.

For the rest of this chapter, David essentially said to stay with God and choose His righteousness. In return, God promised His goodness, safety, and refuge.

Verses 8-22 contain a lot, so look for God's instructions to us. There are more than five, but choose five things we are called to do:

1.
2.
3.
4.
5.

Now look at God's character. What did He promise? Again, there are more than five, but list five:

1.
2.
3.
4.
5.

We can find one of the most quoted verses from Psalm 34 in verse 18: "The LORD is close to the brokenhearted and saves those who are crushed in spirit."

I want you to "wear" this passage as your covering this week. Make this verse yours—both to minister to your own spirit and to be used to minister to others. Sometimes, when I want to apply a passage to my own life, I change the words around something like this:

Angela, the Lord is close to every broken place inside of you, the seen and the unseen. He has not run away. He promises to save you every time your spirit is crushed.

Just writing these few sentences truly ministered to me. I have been crushed so many times, but God keeps saving my spirit. He has already healed some brokenness, and He is still working on some. I know this passage is true. Live in its power today. I want that for you too.

How could you apply verse 18 to your heart today?

As we close up this day, look at the last verse of Psalm 34: "The LORD redeems his servants; no one will be condemned who takes refuge in him" (v. 22).

Every day this week I'm going to remind you that God is our Redeemer. He takes the broken and makes them whole. He makes the old brand-new and the dead come back to life. This is the God we serve. He is I AM. He is to be praised. He condemns none who belong to Him.

What is our instruction in verse 22?

You don't have to learn Greek and Hebrew.
You don't have to know where the Philistines lived or who Achish was.
You don't even have to know all your Bible books in order.
Calling all the broken girls.
Run to God and hide yourself behind His love.
The Lord redeems.
No one will be condemned.

I AM

I AM Refiner.
God is the remover of dross.

I AM Your Husband.
God is providentially caring.

I AM *Jehovah Jireh*.
The Lord who provides.

I AM Redeemer.
The God who delivers the captives.

Broken-Down Jesus Girl

So here I am, a woman who was separated, divorced, lived seven-and-one-half years as a single mom, and just remarried two years ago. A broken-down Jesus girl if there ever was one. I have known broken dreams by the hundreds. My children are growing up in a broken home. Every time I play back these past 10 years and look into the eyes of my beautiful children, my heart breaks all over again.

I could tell you that brokenness has made me a better person, and it has. Or I could tell you that my wounds are almost healed, and they are. But my children—my tender, wonderful children—never did one thing to deserve the brokenness they have suffered so early in their lives. This thing has been awful for all of us, but it grieves me that this is my kids' story too. I cry even as I type these words. I am so very sorry for their pain and the wounds they carry. I meant for them to have the easy life. They have not.

Have others suffered along with you in brokenness? Do you long to see their wounds healed, sometimes even more for them than for yourself?

Just about the time I start to forget what a broken woman I am, someone reminds me, "Well, we won't be able to have another divorced woman speak at our conference." I understand.

"We can't have a divorced woman on the cover of our magazine." Sure, I get it.

"We don't have divorced people on our radio show." It's OK. No problem.

How does this world keep reminding you of your brokenness?

The truth is, I do get it.

We're all looking for the answer. We want to read about the ones who got it right so they can show us the way. There isn't one thing about my past that can be changed. I am absolutely sure that God intended for children to be raised by a mom and a dad who love each other and who live in the same house committed to marriage. But that is not my story, nor will it ever be. The question for me has become, given my circumstances and my brokenness, how now shall I live for the glory of God?

Choosing to live for the glory of God is a choice you make with your heart and your mind. I believe God loves to wrap His glory around the redeemed. He gets all the praise. His name is lifted high.

If you could begin today, what are three new ways you would choose to live for the glory of God?

An elder at my church said to me, "Angela, Jesus was the wounded healer, and I believe that is the ministry He is giving to you." And that is the ministry God *has* given to me. I am so honored to teach the Bible, week after week, all over the world, looking through the lens of my brokenness. It's really OK with me that others would not have me speak at their event. Truly. Deep down. I promise, I'm very OK. I have such an overwhelming gratitude that God would use me to teach His Word to women that nothing inside of me has time to worry about the places I never will be invited to go.

What has your brokenness disqualified you from?

Does that make you feel like you're disqualified from representing God too?

Do you remember our verse yesterday (Ps. 34:18)? Whom is God close to?

Honestly, I'd rather be broken and close to God than whole and far away. The never-been-broken don't know what they're missing!

Most of the e-mails I receive, the letters I get, and little notes that are slipped to me in the book line are from broken women like me. And every one of them says thank you. Thank you for telling the truth. Thank you for standing up. Mostly they say thank you for letting God use you. Are you kidding? Thank me? Goodness, I am so thankful to God that He chooses the broken. I will worship Him with my entire life and spend eternity saying to Him, "Thank You for using a woman like me."

All throughout Scripture we see God as our Rescuer, our Redeemer. His ultimate act of redemption came when He sent His only Son, Jesus, to rescue us from the penalty of our sin and redeem our lives from the bondage of sin. Maybe one of the most poignant stories of this same rescuing, redeeming love is in the Book of Ruth.

Ruth is a little book in the Old Testament where we'll camp for the next few days. Because it's only four chapters long, I'm going to keep today shorter because I'd love for you to take a few minutes and read all four chapters at one sitting.

Let me pray for you,

Father,

I pray for my friend as she sits to read Your Word. Would you give her an ease in this reading, a spiritual understanding, a hunger for more of who You are?

Teach us, Lord.

We love You.

In Jesus' name, amen.

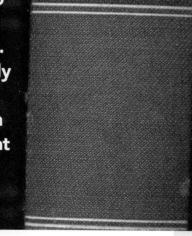

Did you know that God wants to use a woman like you too? He does. They say everybody has at least one book in them with a story to tell. What would the title of your book be?

Ruth and Naomi

The Book of Ruth is a series of struggles, brokenness, redemption, and, ultimately, the glory of God.

We'll start with a quick review: Naomi and her husband had two sons. Because of a famine in their homeland of Judah, they left for Moab. In Moab, Naomi's husband died, leaving her a widowed single mom. The two sons married Moabite women, one named Orpah and the other Ruth. After they had lived there 10 years, both of the sons died. Naomi was left without her husband or sons, living with her two now widowed daughters-in-law.

"Where you go I will go, and where you stay I will stay. Your people will be my people and your God my God. Where you die I will die, and there I will be buried."

RUTH 1:16-17

I want to stop here for a minute and acknowledge that some of you today are living as widows, struggling with the grief of your broken heart and your broken family. I just want you to know you are thought of as I am writing. I am praying that the Spirit of God would be your comfort today.

Maybe you have a widow in your circle of friends or who lives on your street. Today seems like a great day to let her know that you care how she's doing. Maybe you could ask her for dinner or just stop by to check in. Who is someone who could use your hello?

Naomi told the widowed daughters to go back to their families. She could not provide another husband for them, and she was returning to her homeland. She told them she would pray for God to give them new husbands someday. Orpah decided to return to her family, but Ruth spoke to Naomi the oath of her commitment.

You hear this passage quoted at a lot of weddings, and it should be. The commitment it communicates is beautiful. But I love that Ruth spoke these words to her mother-in-law. Already we have a peek into the heart of this special woman. Already I feel myself wanting to be brave and committed like her.

Don't you long to be a woman who grows stronger in character and commitment? We will never get to a place where our character lacks room for improvement. In these six weeks together, how has the Lord been prompting you about strengthening your character? about becoming brave?

So the two widowed women returned to Bethlehem together. Chapter 1 ends with Naomi's bitter grievance toward God: "The Almighty has made my life very bitter. I went away full, but the LORD has brought me back empty. ... The LORD has afflicted me; the Almighty has brought misfortune upon me" (Ruth 1:20-21).

Almost anyone who suffered so much loss would probably grab at her heart and shake her fist at God. Naomi was no different. Such incredible loss had left her completely empty. Her circumstances felt like an affliction. It even felt as if God had brought misfortune to her life.

Have you ever felt as if God were punishing you by keeping you broken?

If our brokenness isn't a punishment from God, where do you think brokenness comes from and why?

Maybe you have known such loss. Maybe your broken heart makes you feel like Naomi, who couldn't find God anywhere in her pain. This story is for women like us who wonder where God is when all hope is gone. It's for the women who wonder where God is when one tragedy after another attacks their faith. It's a story for women who can't imagine that anything good could ever come from their broken lives.

Keep in mind one thing in the hardest times: When it seems everything is falling apart, God's hidden work always remains. When you think God is distant or maybe even He has turned against you, remember that in the unseen, God is plotting for your joy. He is planning the redemption of your brokenness.

The Bible is clear about this. When you believe in Jesus Christ as your Savior, then you are saved—saved from living forever in brokenness. Our brokenness is temporary. Earthly. We will not live for eternity disappointed, rejected, and worn out.

If you have time, read Ephesians 1:1-14; but if not, look at verses 13-14 with me: "*You also* were included in Christ when you heard the word of truth, the gospel of your salvation. Having believed, you were marked in him with a seal, the promised Holy Spirit, who is a deposit guaranteeing our inheritance until the redemption of those who are God's possession—to the praise of his glory." *(Italics mine)*

According to this passage, what happens when you believe?

What is guaranteed?

Through Jesus, we are God's, sealed with the Holy Spirit as a promise of redemption. We face heartache on earth, but brokenness does not win. We have a Redeemer. Because by the power of the Holy Spirit, God will make us whole. We who have been broken will be the praise of His glory!

I completely understand Naomi's bitterness toward God. I understand why you may have felt something similar. But we must not stay in our bitterness. We have a Redeemer. Our future is guaranteed because of the life, death, and resurrection of Jesus. The broken on this earth have the hope of glory.

This Old Testament story of Ruth is what's called a "type of Christ." That's a theological phrase to describe a passage that foretells and pictures the coming Savior. These beautiful four chapters fit together to make a type, a pretelling, of what Christ would come to do for us. Ruth and Naomi were widowed, broken, lost, and even angry. But a Redeemer came into their story, just like God sent His Son Jesus to become our Redeemer.

Don't miss our study time tomorrow; it's going be great. Boaz was on his way to become the kinsman-redeemer for Ruth; but even better, God sent His promised Redeemer for you and for me.

Before we close, remember some things about the One who knows us, the One who is making us brave.

I am worn out ...
  but He is the God who does not grow _____.
I am suffering a thorn ...
  but our God is all-_____.
I am undisciplined ...
  but God promises to be my _____.
I am trembling inside ...
  but God is the God of all _____.
I am invisible ...
  but our God is the God who _____.
I am broken ...
  but oh, hallelujah, God is my _____.

Blessings to you, my friend. We are held, seen, and loved by Almighty God. May that truth give you peace today and make you brave.

Ruth and Boaz

I love a movie with a great ending or a story with a great twist. Today we have come to the part in Ruth's story with the really great, girl-movie kind of ending. As you work through this day, keep in mind that we are promised what Ruth received. Ruth was a broken woman, redeemed. We will be the same.

We pick back up in our story with Naomi and Ruth returning to her homeland of Judah. In Bethlehem, Naomi remembered a relative named Boaz. The Bible calls Boaz a kinsman-redeemer. Old Testament family law gave the kinsman (a close family relative) the right to redeem a relation from slavery or to buy back his fields. Another duty of the kinsman, written about in this story of Ruth, is the obligation of the next of kin to marry a childless widow and have a child to carry on the name of the dead husband. In this way, the line of the family was carried on and the property preserved. Boaz was just the man God had in mind to redeem the broken lives of Ruth and Naomi. He had been working this out in the unseen, plotting for their great, great joy.

As the story goes, Ruth went out during the day to gather fallen grain from various fields, but then "happened" to come to Boaz's field. You're probably already smiling as you realize Ruth didn't just happen onto this godly man's field. God was leading Ruth exactly where He wanted her to be. Nothing is happenstance with God. Boaz was a kind man who showed favor to Ruth even though she was a foreigner. He instructed his men to care for her and never to harm her.

Following the instructions of Naomi, one night during the threshing Ruth came and lay at the feet of Boaz while he slept. This Old Testament custom seems odd to us, but it signaled Ruth's request to Boaz for him to become her kinsman-redeemer.

The next morning Boaz approached the city elders. With wisdom he worked through the process to rescue Ruth and her mother-in-law's land.

Eventually, in the most honorable ways, Boaz became Ruth's kinsman-redeemer. Ruth took her refuge under the protection of the man who came to her rescue. He bought all of Naomi's property and took Ruth as his wife.

> Trust that God is always working in the unseen for your joy, and His glory will transform the timid heart into a brave one.

> "So Boaz took Ruth and she became his wife. Then he went to her, and the LORD enabled her to conceive, and she gave birth to a son.
> The women said to Naomi: 'Praise be to the LORD, who this day has not left you without a kinsman-redeemer. May he become famous throughout Israel! He will renew your life and sustain you in your old age. For your daughter-in-law, who loves you and who is better to you than seven sons, has given him birth.' "
>
> RUTH 4:13-15

Boaz and Ruth were blessed with a son they named Obed. Our God, who is always at work in the unseen places, sovereignly placed this beautiful story of redemption in the lineage of Jesus. Obed became the father of Jesse, and Jesse the father of David, and David continued the direct lineage until the birth of our Savior, Jesus.

Oh my goodness, does it get any better? Well, actually, yes, it does. Remember yesterday I told you that this story is a "type of Christ"? The story of Ruth and Boaz is meant to be a beautiful picture of our relationship with Jesus Christ.

God's love is so deep that He sent a kinsman-redeemer to buy back our lives from the penalty of death. This kinsman-redeemer's name is Jesus, the Son of God, sent from the family of God as your kin. Four Old Testament requirements for a kinsman-redeemer show us that Jesus was the only One qualified to become our kinsman-redeemer.

1. HE MUST BE NEAR OF KIN.

"But made himself of no reputation, and took upon him the form of a servant, and was made in the likeness of men: And being found in fashion as a man, he humbled himself, and became obedient unto death, even the death of the cross" (Phil. 2:7-8, KJV).

God, our Father, sent His Son, Jesus, who was like us in every way except that He never sinned.

Jesus was made in the likeness of

_____,

being found in the fashion of a

_____.

2. HE MUST BE ABLE TO REDEEM.

"For there is one God and one mediator between God and men, the man Christ Jesus, who gave himself as a ransom for all men" (1 Tim. 2:5-6).

Jesus assumed our debt, brokenness, and sin and paid for it with His life. Jesus was the only One able to redeem us. The kinsman-redeemer must have the means by which to pay the debt of the one he redeems. Jesus paid our debt.

What does the reality that Jesus is the one and only Redeemer mean to you?

From these two passages, which phrases tell us that Jesus was willing to redeem?

What kind of relationship or caring would make someone willing to give his or her life for a person?

3. HE MUST BE WILLING TO REDEEM.

"For even the Son of Man did not come to be served, but to serve, and to give his life as a ransom for many" (Mark 10:45).

"The reason my Father loves me is that I lay down my life—only to take it up again. No one takes it from me, but I lay it down of my own accord. I have authority to lay it down and authority to take it up again. This command I received from my Father" (John 10:17-18).

Oh, hallelujah, not only was Jesus able to redeem but He also was willing to come to this earth to become our kinsman-redeemer. He freely gave Himself to redeem us from our iniquity and to purify us so that we might become the beautiful redeemed of God. I love this truth—that Jesus is the sinner's (my) nearest kinsman.

4. REDEMPTION WAS FULLY REALIZED WHEN THE PRICE WAS COMPLETELY PAID.

"In him we have redemption through his blood, the forgiveness of sins, in accordance with the riches of God's grace" (Eph. 1:7).

Jesus' death on the cross bought new life for us. From this Ephesians passage, what have we received?

1.

2.

"He is the atoning sacrifice for our sins, and not only ours but also for the sins of the whole world."

1 JOHN 2:2

Who can be redeemed by the sacrifice of Jesus?

Paid in full. All of our debt was completely paid at the cross. All our shame removed. The gift of life eternal was bought back for us by our nearest kinsman-redeemer, Jesus.

God sent a good man named Boaz to become Ruth and Naomi's kinsman-redeemer. God sent a perfect man named Jesus to redeem each one of our lives from its brokenness, sin, and pain.

> "For all have sinned and fall short of the glory of God. They are justified freely by His grace through the redemption that is in Christ Jesus."
>
> ROMANS 3:23-24, HCSB

A woman in our Bible study was listening to this teaching with tears streaming down her face. Her husband had committed suicide only eight months before. She was still reeling from the shock of becoming a widow and a single mom. She was still angry with the man she had loved so much. She sat with her three girlfriends, and they were all holding hands as we walked through this passage. At this part about Jesus as our kinsman-redeemer, one of the ladies leaned over and wrote on the top of her paper, "Jesus is your Redeemer." All four of those ladies looked at the paper and began to weep openly. Finally, when they could speak, someone told the rest of us the story, and there wasn't a dry eye in the room. It is true for that woman. It is true for me. It is true for you.

Jesus is your Redeemer.

God's mercy takes my breath away.

To Live Like Ruth

I just cannot believe this is our last day together. These past months as I've studied and written, I've prayed for you all along the way. I can't see your face when I pray, but I pray for my *Brave* Bible study girls like we're all best friends. Maybe the best way to describe it is that I hold you in my heart. I think about your struggles as I'm writing. I pray for your children and your marriages. I want God to bring great men for those of you who want to be married. I cheer for my single moms. I wish I could make dinner for all of you, and we'd linger at the table and talk all night about our crazy lives and God who makes us brave.

I think it's fitting that we're wrapping up our time focusing on Ruth. As I've reread this story over and over the past couple of days, I am in awe of several things. First, God is always working in the unseen realm for His glory and to redeem His people. That would include people like you and me. Second, that God would send Jesus to be my kinsman-redeemer takes my breath away. Third, Ruth was a beautiful role model of godliness for all of us. It seems perfect to consider her today. I'd like to look a lot like her.

What other highlights stand out for you this week?

1. RUTH WAS A WOMAN OF COMMITMENT.

Ruth's decision to remain committed to her destitute mother-in-law was incredibly compassionate and amazing. I know you remember when she said to Naomi: "Don't urge me to leave you or to turn back from you. Where you go I will go, and where

> **Our Redeemer pursues, loves, and restores broken women. I want to live every day brave for His glory.**

you stay I will stay. Your people will be my people and your God my God. Where you die I will die, and there I will be buried. May the LORD deal with me, be it ever so severely, if anything but death separates you and me" (Ruth 1:16-17).

What strong, lasting commitments like Ruth's have you made?

Ruth chose Naomi's God and then chose to put her future care into His hands. Ruth committed not only to Naomi but also to the Lord. This passage talks primarily about an earthly relationship, but I can't help but read this passage and consider my own commitment to God, His leadership to me, and His will instead of mine. As you reflect on the consistency of your commitment to God, can you think of three or four adjectives to describe where you are with Him?

Learning from Ruth about commitment means letting my brokenness drive me toward greater commitment and compassion instead of running away from the places where I have known pain.

1.
2.
3.
4.

I want to be:

committed to loving well
the people God has given me to love

_____

committed to being generous with my
heart and compassionate toward others

_____

committed to my God who is working
out His redemption in these things

_____

committed to finishing
my life's journey well

What do you want to be more committed to?

2.
RUTH WORKED WITH HUMILITY.

Old Testament law gave Ruth the right to gather leftover grain from fields that had already been harvested. But instead of presuming it was her right, Ruth went to the foreman of the fields and asked permission.

> *"Please let me glean and gather among the sheaves behind the harvesters."*
> RUTH 2:7

I think brokenness gives a humility we might not have known otherwise. It's the kind of brokenness that teaches us that everything is a gift. That we are not really entitled to anything has been a powerful lesson woven into the past 10 years of my life. Becoming a divorced mom of four was incredibly humbling. Every kindness became a gift. All these years later, I want all that I do to come from that place of humble gratefulness.

What things have taught you the
lessons of humility?

3.
RUTH WAS A VERY HARD WORKER.

The foreman reported to Boaz: "She went into the field and has worked steadily from morning till now" (Ruth 2:7).

I don't know if it's cool these days to be a hard worker, but I am absolutely sure that it's a character trait God rewards. Do you remember this passage?

> *"Whatever you do, work at it with all your heart, as working for the Lord, not for men."*
> COLOSSIANS 3:23

I don't think this means you have to keep doing the very thing you hate to do for the rest of your life. But while you have to, do that work as unto the Lord! Working hard at what the Lord has appointed for you today is cooperating with God. Trusting in His plans. Taking the next step of faith toward the future and the lessons He wants to teach.

4.
RUTH TOOK REFUGE UNDER THE WINGS OF GOD.

Working in the fields of Boaz, Ruth was completely aware that she was a foreigner and a childless widow. When he instructed her to stay in his fields where she would be protected, Ruth asked, "Why have

I found such favor in your eyes that you notice me—a foreigner?" (Ruth 2:10).

"Boaz answered her, 'Everything you have done for your mother-in-law since your husband's death has been fully reported to me: how you left your father and mother and the land of your birth, and how you came to a people you didn't previously know. May the LORD reward you for what you have done, and may you receive a full reward from the LORD God of Israel, under whose wings you have come for refuge'" (Ruth 2:11-12, HCSB).

I love this more than anything! Ruth modeled for us the most perfect place to run with our brokenness— under the wings of God.

If you are struggling with your broken life or broken heart, run to God. Take your shame, embarrassment, pain, and hide yourself in Him. Then, based on everything I have come to know about the family of God, I'd tell you to jump into the center of God's people and stay there. The people of God have been my family. They have prayed for me and strengthened me when I did not have strength on my own. So often they have come or called because "God led them."

Maybe today you need the refuge of God. If you do, I'd love to take you to Him. Maybe you can do something like this:

Find a place to be quiet and alone and then just lie on your face.

I'm praying that the minute you lie down and the room grows quiet, you will sense that God is present. I pray that the first thing you feel in your soul is the overwhelming, enduring love of God. Maybe you can say a prayer like this:

God, I need to hide myself underneath the wings of Your love. Please be my hiding place. Would You protect me and heal me and begin to put all my broken pieces back together? And God, please make me brave.

Let yourself keep praying. Your prayers, not mine. Work from the inside out. Begin with your aching heart and what's hidden inside. Move your prayers out toward your physical body, the world you live in, and the relationships you have.

Let the wings of God keep you safe. Remember His promise from the Book of Joel: He will restore all that the locusts have eaten (Joel 2:25).

Let Him continue the work of healing.

Just pray your life over to God.

Continue to be still after you finish your prayers.

And receive.

Ruth was so much more than the four characteristics we could cover today, but may her life remind us of what we long for:

to live fully committed to the glory of God

———

to live as the redeemed whose stories point to the compassion of God

———

to live as brave women who find their strength hidden underneath the wings of God

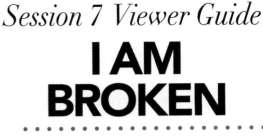

I AM BROKEN

RUTH 4

The question that comes from our brokenness is this:

How now will I live for the _____ of God?

The Book of Ruth: a series of struggles, _____,
redemption, and ultimately the _____ of God.

God is always working in the _____.

The requirements of a kinsman-redeemer:

1. He must be _____ of kin.

2. He must be _____ to redeem.

3. He must be _____ to redeem.

4. Redemption was completed when the _____
   was completely paid.

LEADER GUIDE

· · · · · · · · · · · · · · · ·

Dear Leader,

First, I just want to say thank you. Thank you so much for taking the time to lead this study called *Brave*. I realize that you are giving your energies and your heart to the women in your group, and I want to tell you how grateful I am for your sacrifice and leadership.

Next, I want you to know that even before you read these words, I have prayed for you. I am asking God to give you a beautiful ministry to the women He brings into your circle. May He grant you all the compassion, insight, and tenderness you will need to love each individual woman. Sometimes we think we have to say just the right words when maybe all that's needed is a listening ear, a friend to pray, or a hug for their heartache. Thank you for being there to give what they need. I'm asking God to direct you how to be His sweet minister to each one.

I pray that as you lead, God gives you special wisdom in the application of this teaching. Each group of women is different and varied. May you know, even better than we, how to apply these truths to the lives you touch. May God add new insights as you study together. He is before you and behind you. This work was written for His glory, and I pray He shows off His glory in your midst.

Thank you again, my leader friend. I hope I get to meet you one day and give you a big hug. Live brave, my sister.

With love,

Angela

Thank you for leading the study of *Brave*. This brief leader guide will give you ideas, but rely on the Holy Spirit for guidance. These are only suggestions. The best group results in each member sharing what God has been teaching her for that week. Provide the degree of structure that will fit your group and situation.

The order of print and video in *Brave* differs from some other studies. Women will first study the week of print material on a topic, then watch the video, and finally share in a small group. For the first week your group will watch the session 1 video and do some basic group building. Then members will study week 1 in preparation for group session 2. Since each week's study is complete and on a different topic, you can continue to welcome new members into your group. You could also select from the topics to fit a different schedule as necessary though women would benefit most from working through the entire study together.

In preparation for each week, complete the study and preview the video. Set up the room, including the necessary equipment. Always assure the women that they may decline to share their answers in the group.

SESSION ONE

Use the first session to build fellowship in your group. Familiarize yourself with the topics in *Brave* and preview the study. Explain that members will support each other as you bravely face questions every woman asks. Watch the session 1 video, and ask members for their reaction. Note the viewer guides for the teaching sessions follow each week, but no viewer guide exists for session 1. Here are some additional suggestions:

1. Have women introduce and tell something about themselves.
2. Ask members to list the order of importance they'd give to the six topics in the study (p. 3). Ask which topics they most anticipate and which they most dread.
3. Consider assigning pairs or triads as prayer partners for the duration of the group.
4. Encourage group members to be honest and to absolutely maintain confidentiality as you will be talking about questions that call for courage.
5. Be sure each woman gets a copy of *Brave: Honest Questions Women Ask,* and make the assignment to complete week 1 this week.
6. Pray together that God will make you brave women.

SESSION TWO

Welcome group members and pray. You may begin either by sharing some of the responses to their study this week or by viewing the video. Then, as time permits, discuss some of the following questions on the topic:

1. In what ways do you struggle with worn out? What does worn out feel like to you (p. 8)?
2. How did you complete the sentences on page 9?
3. What are your big three priorities, and what would you like to add (p. 10)?
4. What makes for anxious toil in your life (p. 13)?
5. With which of the causes of worn out do you struggle most (work, anxious toil, grief, sin)?
6. To what things do you think women most often turn with their weariness (p. 17)?
7. With what items do you identify or want to add to your false hope list (p. 19)?
8. To which of the "refreshers" do you most relate (pp. 20-30)?
9. This topic requires balance. God restores us, yet we remain subject to human limitations. How do you maintain that balance? How has God restored you recently? How is He continuing to teach you to wait?
10. How have or might you benefit from observing a regular Sabbath rest?

SESSION THREE

Preview the video in preparation for the session. Get note cards to distribute. Angela will lead the group to anonymously write their thorns on the card as either a physical thorn, a relationship, or something such as an addiction. After the video segment, collect the anonymous cards. Then redistribute them so no one has her own card. Ask them to share the type of thorn on their card and those who do not suffer that type of thorn to pray for those who do. Use wisdom to adjust this to your group.

Welcome group members and pray. As time permits, discuss some of the questions below on the topic of a thorn:

1. Which box or boxes would you check in regard to a thorn (p. 36)?
2. With what feeling have you dealt on your thorn journey (p. 37)?
3. Have you ever received an answer to your why question (p. 38)?
4. How have you struggled believing God's grace is sufficient in a time of pain (p. 39)?
5. How have you tried to remove your thorn? What conclusions have you come to about its place in your life (p. 42)?
6. How has a thorn caused doubts in you (p. 43)?
7. What is God revealing to you about His character (p. 45)?
8. How has a thorn produced weakness in you? How do you feel about it (pp. 49-50)?
9. In what way has a thorn produced humility in your life (p. 52)?
10. What have been your bravest and your most cowardly thorn moments (p. 56)?
11. Review the barbs of the thorn (pp. 41-49). What has God shown you in your study this week? In what ways are you learning to boast in your weakness (p. 60)?

SESSION FOUR

Welcome group members and pray. Either begin by sharing some of the responses to their study this week or by viewing the video. Then, as time permits, discuss some of the following questions on the topic:

1. What items did you put on your undiscipline list (p. 65)?
2. What triggers have you identified that set off the war inside you (p. 66)?
3. What things have you seen exercise control over people you know (p. 69)? What about you? Does something seem to have a hold over you?
4. How do you respond to the holy dependence suggestion—that God may be more concerned with your dependence on Him than on your perfect obedience (p. 74)?
5. In what three tangible ways can you begin training that will lead to discipline (p. 75)?
6. In what areas do you have a little slug potential (p. 77)?
7. Review the 10 ways to begin becoming disciplined (pp. 78-79). Which suggestions do you think you need to apply to your life?
8. What reminds you how human you are and how inconsistent your strength can be (p. 80)?
9. What six ideas can you think of for everyday Jesus girls like us to keep in step with the Holy Spirit (p. 82)?

SESSION FIVE

Welcome group members and pray. Either begin by sharing some of the responses to their study this week or by viewing the video. Then, as time permits, discuss some of the following questions on the topic:

1. Have you ever known the kind of fear that made you tremble (p. 87)?
2. How are the fears of this journey coming at you today (p. 87)?
3. Why do you think Jesus gave the disciples the message in John 16:33 (p. 88)?
4. What do you think it means to "be of good cheer" even though you may be living alongside trouble and trembling on the inside (p. 89)?
5. What does being saved mean to you (p. 90)?
6. From what wrong places or people have you sought comfort (p. 93)?
7. How has your inward suffering turned you outward toward others (p. 97)?
8. What does patient endurance look like in your estimation (p. 98)?
9. Have you ever been under great pressure and despaired for your very life (p. 98)?
10. What is your first response when trouble comes (p. 99)?
11. When you feel forsaken and far from God, which of the six actions from Psalm 22 do you think will be most helpful (pp. 101-102)?

SESSION SIX

Welcome group members and pray. Here are some questions for your group to process together this week:

1. In what ways have you experienced feeling invisible (p. 110)?
2. As you think of the women you know and the life you have lived, what other honest questions do women ask when they feel invisible (p. 110)?
3. How do you secretly play your version of the comparison game (p. 111)?
4. What characteristics of a striving woman would you add to the list (p. 111)? How have you struggled with striving?
5. Have you ever chosen the path of sulking, and if so, what have you learned in the process (p. 112)?
6. How do you see yourself in the story of Sarai and Hagar (p. 113)? To which or both of them do you relate, and in what ways?
7. Can you understand how very real hurt will tell you lies until the mind decides to believe them? What lies have you heard and believed from your pain (p. 114)?
8. What adjectives describe how you feel when someone is happy to see you (p. 117)?
9. Based on what God is doing in your life, what name would you give to Him? What are some ways that we can build modern-day monuments to the glory of God (p. 118)?
10. What five words would you use to describe your perspective of depression (p. 119)?
11. What is one negative connotation you associate with obedience (p. 123)?
12. How does God's good heart toward you shape your attitude of obedience toward Him (p. 124)?
13. How is God asking you to engage your faith today (p. 125)?
14. How does knowing you are never invisible to God help to make you brave?

SESSION SEVEN

Welcome group members and pray. Here are some questions for your group this week:

1. No matter where you are, where you have been, or what you have done, when you look to God, how does He see you (p. 131)?
2. How could you apply Psalm 34:18 to your heart today (p. 132)?
3. How does this world keep reminding you of your brokenness (p. 134)?
4. In what three new ways will you choose to live for the glory of God (p. 135)?
5. They say everybody has at least one book in them with a story to tell. What would the title of your book be (p. 136)?
6. If our brokenness isn't a punishment from God, where do you think brokenness comes from and why (p. 138)?
7. What happens when you believe, and what is guaranteed (Eph. 1:13-14; p. 139)?
8. Of the four characteristics of a kinsman-redeemer (must be closely related, able to redeem, willing to redeem, and the price must be completely paid, pp. 141-142), which attribute means the most to you and why?
9. Of the four descriptions of Ruth (woman of commitment, worked with humility, hard worker, and took refuge in God, pp. 145-147), with which would you most like to identify?
10. What aspect of the story of Ruth impacts you most and why?

Thank you for leading Brave. Encourage your group to celebrate the reality that many times when we least feel brave we are in reality most brave. When we bring the Father our honest questions, He can always be depended on to embrace His daughters and to care for them in His sovereign love.

Endnotes

WEEK 2

1. W. A. Elwell & P. W. Comfort, *Tyndale Bible Dictionary* (Wheaton, IL: Tyndale House Publishers, 2001), 540.
2. I. H. Marshall, et. al. *New Bible Dictionary* (Downers Grove, IL: InterVarsity Press, 1996), 491.
3. W. A. Elwell & P. W. Comfort, *Tyndale Bible Dictionary* (Wheaton, IL: Tyndale House Publishers, 2001), 618.

WEEK 3

1. W. A. Elwell & P. W. Comfort, *Tyndale Bible Dictionary* (Wheaton, IL: Tyndale House Publishers, 2001), 488.
2. John MacArthur, *The Pillars of Christian Character* (Wheaton, IL: Crossway Books, 1998), 139-141.
3. Available from the Internet: *http://www.sermonillustrations.com/a-z/d/discipline.htm*

WEEK 4

1. Matthew Henry, *Matthew Henry's Commentary on the Whole Bible: Complete and Unabridged in One Volume* (Peabody, ME: Hendrickson Publishers, 1991). Available on the Internet: *http://www.biblestudytools.com/commentaries/matthew-henry-complete/john/16.html*
2. Hannah Whitall Smith, *The God of All Comfort* (Westwood, NJ: Barbour, 1984), 34.

WEEK 5

1. W. A. Elwell & P. W. Comfort, *Tyndale Bible Dictionary* (Wheaton, IL: Tyndale House Publishers, 2001), 968.
2. E. M. Bounds, "Prayer and Obedience" public domain. Available from the Internet: *http://www.asermon.com/books/bounds-prayerobedience.html*
3. Ibid.

WE LOVE NEW FRIENDS!

Stop by the LifeWay Women blog.

LifeWayWomen.com

Sign up for our weekly newsletter at lifeway.com/WomensNews